INDIAN ART AND CULTURE

GWA-ESTUMS VILLAGE 1900

INDIAN
ART and CULTURE
of the Northwest Coast

by D. Kew and P. E. Goddard

HANCOCK HOUSE PUBLISHERS

I.S.B.N. 0-919654-13-4

LIBRARY OF CONGRESS CATALOG CARD NUMBER   74-783 41

THIRD PRINTING

Parts of this book were first written by P.
Goddard in 1924.

This edition was edited by D. Kew and has
numerous drawings and photographs that
did not appear in the original edition.

Additional art work has been supplied from
the following sources: THOSE BORN AT
KOONA by John and Carolyn Smyly; and
ARTIFACTS OF THE NORTHWEST COAST
INDIANS by Hilary Stewart for which we
express kind thanks.

KEY TO SOURCE OF ILLUSTRATIONS

British Columbia Provincial Archives	A
Ethnology Division, British Columbia Provincial Museum	E
History Division, British Columbia Provincial Museum	H
British Columbia Department of Travel	T
Edward S. Curtis Collection	C
Hancock House Publishers Library	P
The Coast Indians of Southern Alaska and Northern B.C. by A.P. Niblack	N
Indians of the Northwest Coast by P.E. Goddard	G
Those Born at Koona by John & Carolyn Smyly	S
Wild Berries of the Pacific Northwest by J.E. Underhill	U

The Publishers wish to express their thanks to the above sources.
Photos and art work are described from left to right and from top to
bottom.

PAGE NUMBER:

COVERS, P: 1,A: 2,E: 3,C: 5,S: 6,A,G: 7,A: 8,E,C,E,E,: 9,A,: 10, T,P,P,T,: 12,P,P,P:
13,P,P,P,P: 14,N,E,: 15,G: 16, A,E,E,U: 17,A,E: 18, S,E,: 20,C,N,G,E,: 21,A,E,G,C,C:
22,N,C: 23,E,E,A: 24,N: 25,N: 26,G: 27 E,E,G: 28,E,N,C: 29,N,E,A: 30,A,A,A,E:
31, G,E: 32, G,G,E: 33,E,A,: 34,E,G,: 35,C,P,P: 36,N,G,C: 37,N,C: 38,G: 39,E,A,E: 40,E,G,E:
41,E: 42,P,P,G: 43, C,U,A,A: 44, E,G,G,P,P,P: 45,C: 46, A,C,N: 47,A,C,E,C,A: 48,A: 49,G:
50,N: 51,E: 52,S: 53,S: 54,E: 55,A: 56,N,E,P: 57,E,A,G,S: 58,A: 59,E,C: 60,N: 61,N: 62,P:
63,P: 64,S: 65,E,E: 66,N,C: 67,G: 68,E,A: 69,E,A: 70,A,N: 71,A,E: 72,A: 73,A,G: 74,E: 75,A:
76,A: 78,E: 79,A: 80,N,G,E: 81,N: 82,A,P: 83 P,P,E: 84,E: 85,P,E,E: 86,A,G: 87,E:
88,E,P,A,G,E: 89,G,T: 90,E,G: 91,G,N: 92,A,N: 93, N,A,A,

The publishers also wish to thank the
British Columbia Provincial Archives
for additional historical photographs.

Design by McConnell Design.
Typesetting by White Computer Typesetting,
Vancouver, B.C.

PRINTED IN CANADA

Published by:

HANCOCK HOUSE PUBLISHERS LTD.
10 Orwell Street, North Vancouver, B.C. Canada V7J 3K1 (604)980-4113

CONTENTS

Yukon

Inland Tlingit

JUNEAU

Alaska

TLINGIT

Nass River

Skeena River

TSIMSHIAN

PRINCE RUPERT

HAIDA

QUEEN
CHARLOTTE
ISLANDS

Bella Coola River

**BELLA
COOLA**

Northern
KWAKIUTL

Southern
KWAKIUTL

Fraser River

VANCOUVER

BRITISH COLUMBIA

Washington

PACIFIC

OCEAN

VANCOUVER
ISLAND

NOOTKA

VICTORIA

Makah

**COAST
SALISH**

SEATTLE

N

Quinault

Columbia River

PORTLAND   Oregon

NORTHWEST COAST LINGUISTIC DIVISIONS

HAIDA MEMORIAL POLE

6

INTRODUCTION

Habitat

The Northwest Coast is the land whose aboriginal inhabitants are distinguished by their large rectangular wooden houses and dug-out canoes, scanty dress, and their dependence upon the products of the sea for food. They placed great value upon purity of family descent and the virtue of benevolence in the disposition of property; but most conspicuous of all their traits is their highly original art.

Tribes. Beginning in the northern part of this area, we note the Tlingit tribe, one of the best known divisions of which is the Chilkat. Beyond the Tlingit, along the coast, are the Eskimo who, though resembling somewhat in culture the peoples of the Northwest Coast, are much more closely affiliated, physically, linguistically, and culturally, with the main body of Eskimo. In the interior toward the east the neighbors of the Tlingit, are Athapascan-speaking people. While they have been somewhat influenced by their coast neighbors they may be unhesitatingly classified with their relatives further to the east and in the valley of the Yukon. South of the Tlingit are the Haida, who in many respects may be regarded as typically of the Northwest Coast culture. Their neighbors on the east are the Tsimshian-speaking tribes of closely similar culture, living mainly on the Nass and Skeena rivers, their villages extending for quite a distance up these rivers into a somewhat different environment and a less humid climate; they maintained, however, a life quite similar to that of the coast people, securing through trade those products which are naturally limited to the sea. East of the Tsimshian are Athapascan tribes, strikingly different from them in nearly every respect.

As we proceed southward, the tribes become different both in appearance and in mode of life. It will be more convenient to discuss them by referring first to their language. They belong to two separate linguistic stocks: the Wakashan and the Salish. The former consists of two dialectic groups, the Kwakiutl and Nootka; the main body of the Kwakiutl live on the northern part of Vancouver Island, the neighboring smaller islands, and the adjacent mainland to the east. Geographically isolated to the north are two Kwakiutl dialects: the Haisla and the Heiltsuk, the best known tribes belonging to these groups being the Bella Bella, living on Fitzhugh Sound and the Kitlope on Gardiner Channel. They are separated from the other Kwakiutl and closely affiliated with a Salish-speaking people, the Bella Coola, who live on Burke Channel and its extensions. The Nootka are confined to the west coast of Vancouver Island, unless one includes with them the Makah, a tribe closely related in speech, living on the American side of the Straits of Juan de Fuca.

CHIEF WITH SPEAKER'S STAFF

KWAKIUTL

KWAKIUTL

THE PEOPLE

KWAKIUTL

The main body of the Salish, from whom the Bella Coola have become separated, occupy a large and continuous area in southern British Columbia and the western portion of the State of Washington. They occupy the eastern part of Vancouver Island, south of Cape Mudge, and the southern end of the Island around Victoria. On the mainland of British Columbia and the State of Washington the boundaries are less definite. Salish-speaking peoples live along the Fraser River and occupy its large tributary, the Thompson River. These interior Salish tribes, the Thompson, Lillooet, and Shuswap, have never been considered as possessing the culture of the coast peoples since their houses, dress, food, religion, and art, are quite different not only from those of the Northwest Coast, but from their other neighbors as well.

In respect to such traits as rectangular houses, canoes, dress, food in part, and the regard for birth and wealth, there is an extension of the northwest culture southward down the coast of Washington and Oregon and into California, as far as Humboldt Bay.

TLINGIT

KWAKIUTL

8

NOOTKA

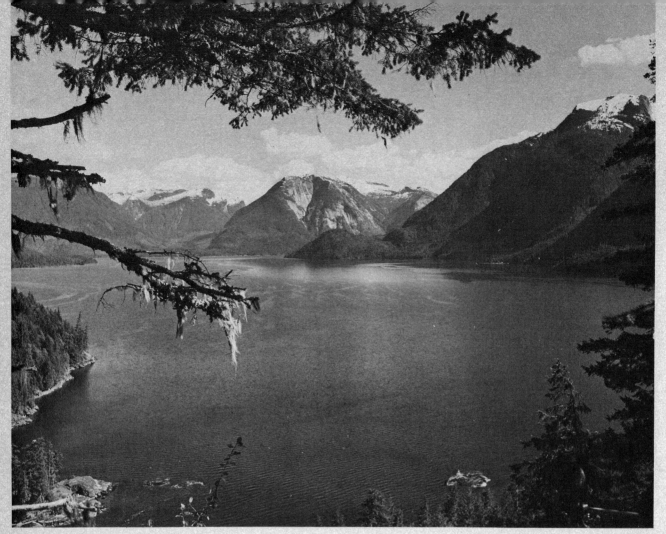

THE INNER COAST

THE LAND

THE OUTER COAST

10

Topography. In many respects the northern Pacific coast of America resembles that of Scandinavia. Both regions have been subject to remarkable depression, so that the valleys are flooded by the sea and the mountains rise abruptly from the water. Long arms of the ocean cut deeply into the land and the streams flowing into them are usually rushing mountain torrents. The heavy precipitation results in the steep mountains being covered with forests or snow.

On the whole, the northwest coast of America is an exceedingly favorable region for the development of a culture almost entirely dependent upon canoes for travel and transportation and upon the sea for its food supply. The sheltered channels are so continuous that the larger dug-out canoes can be brought quite safely from Skagway, at the mouth of the Chilkat River, to the southern end of Puget Sound, provided the weather is favorable for crossing the two or three more exposed stretches of water.

Because of the broken nature of the seacoast, the waterways formed the natural highways of travel so that, with the exception of a few trails which crossed to the interior, there was little travel by land. Nearly everywhere the native settlements were on the ocean shore or along the navigable rivers. Vancouver Island was crossed by trails at several places, one was from the head of Alberni Sound to the east coast, another was from Nimkish Lake to Kyukuot and Nootka sounds, and a third led from Fort Rupert to Quatsino Sound.

Farther north were the so-called "grease trails" used by trading parties, particularly in bartering for eulachon oil.

Flora. The whole region, from California northward, was heavily forested, with hemlock, Douglas fir, spruce, and cedar; yellow cedar was more prevalent in the north and red cedar in the south. Along rocky points where it is difficult for large trees to maintain themselves, madronas or arbutus and a few oaks are found. In the river bottoms are large areas where alder and cottonwood predominate. Everywhere in the forest there is a heavy undergrowth of blueberry and huckleberry bushes, of vine maple, thimbleberries, and salmon berries. This density of vegetation is directly related to the heavy rainfall. Ferns tend to take the place of grasses which are practically unknown, except in the swamps, but a heavy growth of moss forms a thick carpet underfoot and covers the branches of trees.

THE GREAT FORESTS

THE COASTAL FIORDS

11

Fauna. The fauna of the area varies considerably. Of land mammals the most important are deer, elk, mountain goat, and along the courses of the northern rivers, moose. Bear were also plentiful throughout the entire region, although the grizzly and brown bear were common only in the north. Sea mammals were of much greater importance to the economic life than land mammals; the chief of these were the whale, seal, sea-lion, and porpoise. The sea-otter was an important source of clothing and in later years, a source of trade wealth.

Above all, however, the natives of the Northwest Coast depended for their chief food supply on fish, especially the salmon which was the great staple in the whole region. Each spring the salmon ascended the rivers to spawn and at this time the year's supply was obtained. A variety of salt water fish, such as cod, halibut, herring, eulachon, and smelt, were important additions to the fish diet. Especially in the south, shellfish such as clams, oysters, mussels, and crabs were of considerable importance.

THE WILDLIFE

KILLER WHALES

SEA OTTERS

MOUNTAIN GOATS

BLACK BEAR CUB

MOUNTAIN LION

STELLER'S SEA-LIONS

DETAILS OF HAIDA HOUSE CONSTRUCTION, PLUS FRONTS OF OTHER NORTHWEST COAST HOUSES.

MAMALILIKULA HOUSE, KWAKIUTL, 1917

MATERIAL CULTURE

Information concerning the food, clothing, housing, and industrial arts of primitive peoples is grouped under the heading of material culture. For the Indians of the Northwest Coast, their material culture may be characterized by large dependence upon sea food; extensive use of cedar, the wood for houses, canoes, utensils, etc., the bark for mats and woven costumes; and the absence of pottery and agriculture. It is not far wrong to say that these Indians used cedar for everything possible. Their skill in building houses, hollowing out canoes from large tree trunks, bending and joining wood to make boxes and other containers, commands our admiration. Large planks were split from cedar logs, the surfaces of which were dressed smooth with hand adzes. The totem poles, house posts, canoes, and other wooden objects fully illustrate the expertness of these Indian workmen.

METHOD OF ERECTING HOUSE POSTS. KWAKIUTL.

Houses

Salish. The houses of the southern group of tribes, including the Salish of the Fraser River Delta and the Nootka of the west coast of Vancouver Island, were long and rectangular in groundplan with a roof sloping downward to the rear walls which are lower than the front walls. Those of the Kwakiutl and of the northern tribes were more nearly square, varying considerably in size from twenty by thirty feet up to fifty by sixty. A feature common to the houses of all the tribes of the area is an independent inner main framework and an outside covering or shell. The framework persisted from year to year, even from generation to generation, while the planks of the outer shell might have been removed and transported to other localities annually or might be pulled down and afterward replaced at the death of the house owner. The framework of the southern houses consisted of a double row of posts two or three feet wide and from five to eight inches thick. These posts were paired along either side; separated according to the desired width of the house. Those forming the rear of the house were of a lesser height than the posts at the front. Atop these posts were placed long beams which served to support the roof boards, providing a very gentle slope for the roof. Such houses were enclosed with split planks, placed horizontally between pairs of vertical poles, lashed together with withes to hold them in place. The slightly sloping roof was made by overlapping planks which ran lengthwise of the house. These southern houses were built with the higher long side facing the beach. The entrance or entrances were ordinarily on the seaward side with an exit also in the rear.

METHOD OF RAISING HOUSE BEAMS.

ROOF BOARD CONSTRUCTION.

A house of this sort was occupied by a large number of families, each with its separate fire. Ordinarily, each family was assigned the

SALISH ENCAMPMENT, FRASER RIVER.

space between two pairs of the separating puncheons. Raised platforms ran along inside the house against the walls which were hung with mats. The various sections of the house were also separated during the winter season by suspended mats. Household property was stored on and under the side platforms where sleeping places were also provided. The household fires, instead of being in the center of each section, were built in one corner of it, toward the front where the roof was highest. For potlatch occasions a high platform was provided outside at one end of the house from which property was distributed.

Nootka. Nootka houses of this same general style were described by the earlier writers. As among the Salish, the pattern of framework and the placing of the planks varied somewhat from one group to another.

Kwakiutl. The groundplan of a Kwakiutl house was laid out with a cedar rope, a line was first run from the middle of the front to the middle of the back. By doubling the rope, the distance from these middle points to the corners was easily measured. A rectangle was then secured by making the distances equal from each corner to the middle of the opposite side. The typical Kwakiutl house-frame consisted first, of two large posts fifteen to twenty feet long and two feet in diameter. These were set up six feet apart and about three feet back of what was to be the front line of the house. Across the top of these two posts a short beam was placed in semicircular depressions

TLINGIT HOUSE, 1902.

KWAKIUTL HOUSES, 1900.

provided for it. At the rear of the house two similar posts with the same spacing were erected, but ordinarily without the cross-beam. Next was provided a pair of horizontal beams as long as the full depth of the house, often fifty or sixty feet in length and eighteen inches in diameter. They were nicely adzed, and slightly fluted, with the adze marks left unobliterated for their decorative effect.

These houses stood with the gable end toward the sea and had a door of moderate height near the middle. At the rear end of the house, the more desirable location, were the sleeping quarters for the owner's family, generally enclosed by a plank wall. At the rear, on the right was often a similar enclosure for the safe-keeping of ceremonial objects. This served also as a dressing room when ceremonies were in progress. Along the sides were the sleeping places of the other inmates. Each house fire was partitioned off with mats, and had a rack above it for the storage and drying of fish.

Chilkat. The houses of the northern tribes of this area were ordinarily not so large as those of the Kwakiutl. At Klukwan, a Chilkat (Tlingit) village, were rectangular houses, with longitudinal wall planks which fitted into grooves in the corner posts and in an additional post placed midway of the sides.

The houses of some of the chiefs seem to have been provided with a series of earthen banks inside, forming a terrace. Many of the northern houses have carved poles placed against the middle of the front end with the house entrance through an opening cut in them.

INSIDE NOOTKA HOUSE

INSIDE HAIDA PIT HOUSE.

17

SKEDANS VILLAGE, HAIDA, 1878

KWAKIUTL CANOES.

Canoes

Travel on the Northwest Coast was almost entirely by water. The cedar furnished an ideal wood for the construction of canoes, trees of this species often providing logs sufficiently large to build canoes of sixty or more feet in length. The wood of the cedar is soft and easily worked, yet, it is at the same time very resistent to decay. Although canoes for from one to four persons were easy to build, it was a long and difficult task to construct the larger transport and war canoes. There was a difference in type between the canoes of the northern and southern tribes of the area: in the northern type both the bow and the stern were raised and projected over the water; in the southern type, used by the Nootka and Salish, the canoe had a vertical stern and projecting bow. The canoes with projecting bows were particularly used in still protected waters; on the rivers, smaller canoes, of much the same pattern were used. Most of the tribes also constructed rather rough undifferentiated "knockabouts."

PADDLES

The size varied from those not more than eight feet in length and carrying only one man to the great ocean-going canoes seventy feet long and capable of carrying fifty or sixty men. With such canoes the Haida visited as far south as Puget Sound, seven or eight hundred miles from their home.

These canoes were propelled with paddles having a lanceolate blade and a crutch-like handle. A somewhat longer paddle was used by the steersman in controlling the direction of the craft. Canoes were also sometimes sailed, perhaps even before contact with Europeans. The sails were made either of very thin planks lashed to a framework or of matting. In very rough weather the Nootka, at least, were accustomed to attach seal-skin floats to the gunwales of the canoes to give greater buoyancy.

CANOES, VICTORIA.

KWAKIUTL CANOES.

TLINGIT CANOES.

CANOE BAILERS

KWAKIUTL CANOE

SALISH CANOE

TYPICAL FAMILY OR TRANSPORTATION CANOES.

WEDDING GUESTS ARRIVE. KWAKIUTL.

GOING TO THE POTLATCH

ADZING OUT CANOE, CHURCHOUSE. SALISH

SALISH CANOES OUTSIDE FRASER RIVER FISH CAMP.

23

ADZE

CHISELS WITH BONE BLADES. KWAKIUTL.

STONE MAULS.

Work in Wood

The Northwest Coast peoples excelled in woodwork. There is no other region in the world which provides at once so abundant and so satisfactory species of trees for the manufacture of articles which in the other parts of the world are made of bark or skin. Woodwork as it developed on the Northwest Coast had some unique features, such as the steaming and bending of boards to facilitate box-making.

Tools. The woodworking tools were of polished stone, shell, antler, and bone. They had no axes, but had two forms of adzes. One of these had the blade attached to a piece of wood from the trunk of a tree with a section of the attached limb forming an angle, furnishing a handle about two feet long. In the other kind, the blade was attached to a rectangular piece of wood, much like the handle of a carpenter's saw. The blades were of shell, bone, or stone. Chisels had wooden handles and, before metals were common, stone or bone blades.

Felling. Usually, it was not necessary to cut down standing trees since storms and floods furnished a sufficient supply of logs. When such logs were not available, trees were felled or slabs were split from a standing live tree. For the splitting of planks, a scarf was cut with a stone adze or chisel at the base of the tree at the side that promised the best material. In this hole a fire was built and kept under control. Then, by building a platform, workmen were able to make cuts into the tree at a height which was determined by the length of plank desired. Here he made two cuts about eighteen inches apart. The section between these cuts was split out and then wedges were driven in splitting off a long plank of the desired thickness. It seems to have been the general practice along the Northwest Coast to explore the tree first by chiseling a hole in it to make certain it was entirely sound.

Splitting Planks. Trees already on the ground, either selected from the ocean drift or windfalls, or those that had been chopped down, were severed at the desired place by building over them a fire in which stones were placed to localize the heat. Water applied on either side of the fire prevented its spreading beyond the desired limits. The log so cut off was split with wedges. Among the Kwakiutl seven wedges of graduated lengths, were always set in a row across the end of a log. The longest wedge was the farthest from the workman. With a stone hand-hammer the wedges were tapped in succession until the log was split. It is claimed that the direction of the split along the length of the log was controlled somewhat by manipulating the internal stresses, either by loading the log with stones, or by rolling it until its own weight became effective. Even a small log would furnish several planks of the desired thickness. For some purposes planks were split radially and for other purposes with the normal contours of the rings followed across the plank. The split planks were afterward reduced to the required thickness and smoothness, with chisels, adzes, and abrasives. A hand adze was employed for further smoothing. The adzing was either carried along the length of the plank with the grain, giving a fluted appearance; or across its width, giving a rippled effect. If a perfectly smooth surface was desired, grit stones and shark's skin were employed to remove the adze marks.

KNIVES.

WEDGES

HAND ADZES WITH STONE BLADES.

Bending Wood. Wood was successfully bent for several purposes. The making of boxes was a particularly ingenious process. A board, split through the heart of the tree, and of a sufficient length to reach around the perimeter of the proposed box, was worked down to a uniform thickness with a chisel and an adze. It was carefully measured with measuring sticks made for the particular purpose, and kerfs were then cut, with the necessary bevel on one side as shown in the illustration. When the board was ready, ditches were dug in the earthen floor of the house, spaced to correspond to the kerfs in the board, which was laid down and hot stones placed below and above the kerfs. Eel grass was then spread over the stones, water poured on, and mats spread over the whole board. When the steam so generated had done its work, wooden clamps, provided for the purpose, were slipped on the board and brought to the edge of the kerf and the board bent to a right angle. When the board had been bent three times, the sides of a square or rectangular box were provided. The board was held in this position by a rope of cedar withes, until diagonal holes had been drilled through the corner, where their ends met. Wooden pegs were driven into these holes, or spruce root passed through them, to sew the ends together. A bottom was provided and a groove cut around its edges into which the sides fitted. This bottom was attached to the sides either by pegging or sewing. Many of the boxes were also provided with covers.

Boxes of this sort were used for cooking food by means of hot stones, for water vessels, and for storage. Finally, when death occurred one of the larger boxes was used as a coffin into which the body was placed.

Steaming was also resorted to in producing the abruptly curved fish-hooks used for halibut and cod. Those of the southern tribes were made from the knots where the limbs joined the trunk, worked down to the desired size, and then placed inside a kelp stem. This was buried over night in the hot ashes of the fire. The next morning the pieces were bent to the desired curve and forced into a wooden mold, made by digging a groove with the proper curvature in the surface of a board. When the hooks had set in this mold they were removed, warmed by the fire, rubbed with tallow, and then returned to the mold. The tallow was said to prevent their straightening out in the future.

WOODEN STORAGE BOXES—BOARD IS CUT FOR FOLDING.

Dugout Dishes. Food-serving dishes were usually made of alder since this wood would not impart a flavor to foods. When a piece of suitable length had been split out, the side nearer the heart of the tree was adzed and shaped for the bottom of the vessel; the outer side was excavated until the sides of the dish were of the required thickness. For feasts very large vessels of this sort were provided, often carved in the form of a person or an animal.

Canoe-making. The construction of a canoe with primitive tools was a formidable undertaking. When a log of the proper length and size had been secured, the outside was adzed to the approximate shape desired. The inside was excavated, partly by adzing, and partly by the fire which was allowed to char the wood slightly. The charred portion was easily removed and the operation repeated. The thickness of the sides was judged, either by running the hands over the outside and inside and noting irregularities; or by boring holes through the sides, taking measurements and later plugging the holes. The canoe was given a greater width than the diameter of the tree from which it was made, by partially filling it with water which was heated by dropping in hot stones. Cross-pieces were then forced in to spread the canoe which was later held to that shape by thwarts sewed to the gunwales. The stern and bow pieces were made of separate pieces and, sometimes the gunwales were raised by planks, which were sewed on.

Sewing Wood. Joining wood by sewing must be considered one of the special accomplishments of the Northwest Coast people. The conception may have been taken over from birchbark work by the interior tribes, but nevertheless great skill was shown in the application of this technique to woodwork. The spruce root threads were often concealed in deep grooves so as to be unnoticed in the finished product. Mending of cracks in canoes and other objects was by an ingenious use of sewing.

CORNER JOINT, SEWN.

CRADLE WITH CEDARBARK BEDDING.

WATER BUCKET

STORAGE BOXES.

FEAST DISH

OIL DISHES.

STORAGE BOXES.

CEREMONIAL SPOON.

Basketry and Textiles

The textile products of the Northwest consisted of nets, mats, baskets, and blankets. As in other phases of life, the tribes of the southern and northern portions of the territory may be differentiated from those of the middle sections.

Nets. Nets were usually made of nettle fiber. The nettles were cut in October and dried for five or six days out-of-doors and then over the house fire. When the stems were thoroughly dry they were somewhat shredded and the fibers combed out. The women spun the nettle fiber with the aid of a spindle; the raw material was draped over a stake, and the fiber, while in process of spinning, coiled in a box of sand. The strands were combined and re-combined to produce two and four-ply twine, according to the size and strength required. The net was made by tying the twine in meshes of uniform size which was determined by the use of a mesh measure. The long eulachon nets were conical with a mouth opening about six feet in diameter, tapering to the smaller end.

Mat Making. The methods of manufacture for mats as well as the finished products were quite uniform for the entire area. The material was either the inner bark of the red cedar or the much softer bark of the yellow cedar, varying with the prevalence of the tree. The cedar-bark was divided into strips of appropriate thickness and width and then plaited either in a plain checker, or diagonally in a twill. While in progress, the work was suspended from a bar placed horizontally at a height convenient for the woman to work when seated. The warp strands were draped over this bar so that they hung evenly on either side. To secure them in position two strands of bark were twined across the upper edge. A dish of water was always at hand to keep the material sufficiently damp to be pliable.

HAIDA WOMAN, WEAVING HAT.

GILLNET

DIPNETS

GILLNETTING SALMON.

28

In the southern portion of the area along the Fraser River reeds were available for mat making. These were fastened together by passing a string directly through them at intervals.

Basketry. For certain types of basket the prevailing technique was in open work twining. Warp strands, usually of split spruce root, were interwoven in checker work to form the bottom and were then continued upward to serve only as a warp. The weft consisted of two sets of smaller and more pliable root material. One of these was placed horizontally along the inside of the basket and the second wrapped around the first between each warp strand and then carried outside the warp strand diagonally, firmly binding the two together. Such baskets are of open-work and the weft strands are spaced so as to give the desired openness. A basket of very pleasing appearance was produced by arranging the warp strands so that they run diagonally up the basket in opposite directions so as to cross. Two strands of the same material are twined around horizontally engaging these warp strands.

CEDAR BARK BASKETS AND HAT

SPRUCE ROOT HAT

KWAKIUTL WOMEN WITH WOVEN BASKETS AND BED ROLL.

BASKET WEAVER.

29

MAKAH BASKETS.

SALISH BASKETS.

CHIEF'S DAUGHTER TENDS BASKETS.

NOOTKA WEAVER.

30

BARK SHREDDERS.

BARK BEATER

Tlingit Baskets. The northern Tlingit developed a great variety of ornamented baskets of twined weave. The material employed by the Tlingit in constructing these baskets was obtained from the smaller roots of the Sitka spruce. As soon as the roots were gathered the bark was removed by carefully roasting the roots and pulling them through a split stick. The roots were then divided: the outer portions, smooth and shiny, were used for the weft, the inner layers for the warp; the hearts were discarded. These roots were gathered in the spring or summer and seasoned until winter which was the proper time for basket-making. Three kinds of twining were employed: plain two-strand twining; three-strand twining when strength was desired at the turn of the basket where the walls begin; and two-strand twining over pairs of warp strands, which were re-grouped in the succeeding rows to give a diagonal effect.

The ornamentation was produced by over-laying the weft with grass or maiden-hair fern stems. The grass was either bleached and used white or dyed. The material was dyed black by burying it for a time in certain types of black mud or by steeping it in an infusion of hemlock bark. Yellow dye, made from tree moss or from the roots of Oregon grape was also employed, as well as red from an alder vessel in which urine had been allowed to stand. A purple was produced from huckleberries. Like nearly all textile designs these naturally resulted in geometrical patterns. Esthetically, these are among the most pleasing of North American Indian baskets. The technical execution is excellent, the colors harmonize, and spacing is nicely arranged. Formerly, they were made for household use; for cooking, for water, and for storing food, varying in size and form according to these requirements.

Cedarbark Blankets. Several tribes wove blankets and capes of fiber made from the bark of the cedar. The inner bark was taken from the tree in July and soaked for ten days by weighing it down in still, shallow, salt water. It was then beaten across the grain by an implement, made from the bone of a whale, in shape and appearance like the Polynesian tapa beaters. For weaving, a frame was erected, consisting of two stakes set up vertically at the required distance from each other to the top of which was tied a horizontal bar, provided with a groove on its lower edge. A strip of cedarbark was then fastened to the two stakes and attached just under the horizontal bar. The warp of soft cedarbark was draped over this line which was then pressed into the groove in the horizontal bar and bound tightly in place. The warp fibers were separated into small units, each of which became a warp strand. The weft consisted of two strands which were twined across horizontally. The blankets and capes were given the desired shapes by inclining the tops of the posts toward each other, and, by making the warp strands in the middle longer than those at the two edges. Yarn of mountain goat wool was used for the border of these fabrics which in earlier days were also bound with strips of sea-otter fur.

WOMAN SHREDDING BARK. KWAKIUTL.

Chilkat Blankets. The Chilkat of Lynn Canal carried the weaving of mountain goat wool to a very high development. The skins of three animals were required to give sufficient wool for one blanket. The skins were soaked until the wool and hair loosened and could be easily pulled off. The coarse hair was discarded and the wool spun between the palm of the hand and the thigh. Two-strand yarn was made for the weft. The warp was prepared by enclosing a strand of cedarbark with a strand of goat wool yarn. Three colors were employed in dyeing yarn for the weft: Black was obtained from hemlock bark and yellow from the tree moss, *Evernia vulpina.* Decoctions were made of these in urine and the wool boiled in them for some hours and allowed to steep much longer. A green blue was secured by allowing copper to corrode in urine and boiling wool in the resulting liquid.

The loom was similar to that used for weaving the cedarbark blankets described above. The posts, however, were placed in heavy wooden blocks instead of in the ground. The warp strands were cut in several lengths and then sorted and arranged to give the finished blanket the desired curve at the bottom. The long warp strands of a newly commenced blanket were gathered in bundles and placed in bags to keep them out of the way and also to keep them clean. Simple two-strand twining was first employed and then three-strand twining. In the body of the blanket two-strand twining was so manipulated as to produce a diagonal effect. This is accomplished by including two warp strands between each twist and the crossing of the weft strands, and the next time pairing the warp strands differently. The colored weft strand was not carried entirely across the web, but only to the edge of a unit of the pattern. The designs were composed of the usual conventionalized and semi-religious motives of the region. Since the women were not supposed to be familiar with them they were drawn on a board by some man. The blankets being nearly always bilaterally symmetrical, it was considered sufficient to draw the pattern to include only the middle and one side of the board. While these blankets were woven only by the Chilkat, at least in modern times, they are possessed as objects of wealth by most Northwest Coast tribes and worn on ceremonial occasions.

DETAILS OF SUSPENDING CHILKAT BLANKET.

Designs on Chilkat Blankets

CHILKAT BLANKETS.

WOMAN SPINNING MOUNTAIN GOAT WOOL.

Salish Blankets. The Salish peoples of the south, particularly on the lower Fraser River, made blankets of a type quite different from those of the Tlingit. In addition to the mountain goat wool they had a supply derived from white woolly dogs bred for the purpose. The wool was mixed with diatomaceous earth and beaten to remove the grease and make the fibers adhere more readily in the spinning, which was done between the palm of the hand and the thigh. The spun threads were twisted into two-strand yarn with the aid of a spindle which had a large decorated whorl. To secure the desired tension, the threads were drawn over a beam or other handy object. Feathers were also combined with the wool in spinning. The loom consisted of two uprights into which two horizontal rollers were fitted. By the use of uprights of varying heights, a web of any desired size could be made. The rollers were wedged apart to give the needed tension to the warp. The warp threads were not carried spirally around the two rollers, but were passed around a tightly drawn cord or a stick and then doubled back so that when the web was finished and the cord or stick withdrawn, the fabric would separate into a single piece with four selvages. When weaving, the woman sat in front of the loom with a ball of weft which she passed through the shed, beating it down with a comb. As the work progressed she drew the warp around the rollers, after loosening the wedges which held them in place. In weaving the warp strands were usually grouped in pairs, producing a diagonal appearance. Occasionally ornamentation was attempted by the use of color, black or brown, introduced as stripes into the warp. The diagonal treatment then produced narrow bands broken with alternate white and colored lines having an upward and downward slope.

HAIDA WEAVER.

PAUL KANE PAINTING OF SALISH WEAVER MAKING BLANKET.

DEAD WHALES ABOUT TO BE CUT UP.

Food Gathering

Probably no region of the world excelled the Northwest Coast in abundance and variety of marine life. It was largely from this source that the tribes of this area derived their food supply. At certain seasons of the year the sea and rivers literally teem with salmon and this fish was the staple article of diet, corresponding in that respect to maize among the Pueblo tribes or to buffalo among the Indians of the Plains. Other species of fish, as well as shellfish and sea mammals occur in great abundance throughout the area, but these were of lesser importance in the diet of these people. Further variety in foodstuffs was supplied by land mammals and by such plant foods as berries, roots, and barks. These almost limitless supplies of food resulted in a complete absence of periods of famine. The comparative ease with which it was possible to secure an adequate supply of food during a few months of the year probably accounts for the exuberance of the ceremonial life during the somewhat idle winter months.

Whaling. The food of the people of the Northwest Coast was chiefly drawn from the sea, but again distinction may be made between the various portions of the area. The Nootka, of the southern section, had one outstanding achievement not common to the other tribes. They and some of their neighbors to the south pursued and killed whales, while the northern tribes were content with those which were stranded or cast up on the beach. Usually it was the California gray whale which was taken. The chief harpooner was a man of distinction, who inherited the position, and was under many restrictions regarding his food and social behavior. In particular, at the proper season he withdrew to a certain "house" consisting only of posts and poles and not enclosed or covered with planks. In this were many wooden figures of men and the skulls of his ancestors. Here he kept his vigils and engaged in prayer for success. The equipment for whaling consisted of canoes capable of accommodating eight men and sufficiently sturdy to be taken well outside the sheltered inlets. The harpoons had a head with a broad triangular metal or shell blade, antler barbs, and a shaft of yew wood ten feet long, tapering from the middle toward each end. The lines consisted of a leader

SEAL SKIN FLOAT

of whale sinew and sections of rope made from cedar withes. Floats were attached. The outer end of the shaft was inserted in the harpoon head which became detached as soon as the whale was struck.

The harpooner aimed at a spot just behind the front flipper of the whale. As soon as the whale was struck, the crews of the other canoes were permitted to throw as many harpoons as possible. The movements of the whale were impeded by the many attached sealskin floats and he was readily dispatched with lances. The floats, sometimes forty to fifty in number, prevented the sinking of the dead whale which was towed to a beach at or near the village. The "whale chief," who threw the first harpoon, was entitled to a piece of blubber from the back between the head and the dorsal fin. This was decorated with feathers and supported by two stakes and a cross-piece until such time as it was convenient to have a feast. The remainder of the whale was cut up and distributed, the blubber being divided into sections about two feet square. Practically the entire animal was consumed or utilized in some way. The black skin was eaten, the sinews used for ropes, and the digestive organs employed as containers for oil. The Nootka, as well as the other tribes who did not pursue whales, gladly made use of any animal which was stranded on the shore. The Nootka took sea-lions in a manner similar to that described above for whaling. Harpooning sea-lions was an inherited duty, the position of harpooner being second in honor to that of the chief.

Hunting Porpoises. Porpoises were taken with a harpoon. The Kwakiutl used a special canoe made and afterward kept as smooth as possible, and never dragged on the ground or allowed to grate on the shore. It was greased with tallow and scented with spruce boughs. The crew consisted of a steersman and a harpooner who directed the operations, communicating with the steersman by signs. Great care was taken to make no noise in paddling. The harpoon was two-pronged, with detachable barbed heads, fastened to a long line. A float was attached to the line. When a porpoise had been approached within striking distance, a harpoon was thrown, and the canoe backed to avoid the wounded animal, which dove and rose again near the same spot. The canoe was then brought close to the animal which was thrust through the body with a harpoon handle or a long lance. Usually several canoes engaged in such a hunt encircled the victim.

Sealing. Seals were hunted in much the same manner as porpoises. Great care was exercised after harpooning to prevent the seal from swimming through kelp or seaweed and entangling the line which would then be broken or pulled loose. The hunters continually drove him under water with the harpoon pole until the animal was nearly or quite drowned. A blow with a club finished him. The seal hunters knew where the seals customarily slept. When the seals took to the water, the harpooner thrust into the phosphorescence under the water and secured the seal before he had time to escape. Seal meat was highly prized and much used in the feasts.

NOOTKA WHALER

WHALE AHEAD

HARBOR SEAL.

HALIBUT HOOKS.

FISH CLUBS.

FISH JIGS.

Fishing. Many varieties of fish flourished in the ocean and its inlets. Chief among these were the halibut, cod, herring, salmon, and eulachon. The particular local conditions determined which of these fish held the first place as food. In certain regions the halibut was of special importance. There are excellent banks in Queen Charlotte Islands. The Haida and Kwakiutl, therefore, made great use of halibut. The method of taking these fish was everywhere the same. Large hooks were used, those of the Kwakiutl having been constructed by bending a fir or hemlock stick as described above. Farther north, a V-shaped hook was made, and ornamented by carving. A barb of sharp bone or antler was baited with a piece of squid. The hook was attached to a line made of twisted kelp stem, about one-quarter of an inch in diameter, and very strong when wet. The other end of the line was attached to a float; and a sinker rested on the bottom, steadying the hook and holding it in a vertical position. The Kwakiutl were accustomed to set these hooks in pairs so that only one sinker and one float were required for the two hooks. When the huge fish took the bait, the outer curves or prongs of the hook passed outside of its mouth and served as a lever to drive the barb deep into its flesh. In the accounts of the earlier voyages, great praise is given to this device which the white seamen themselves adopted with profit.

The fish were cleaned on the shore by the women, who cut off the heads and tails for separate treatment. The skin was also removed and dried separately from the flesh which was thinly sliced for drying. The heads and tails were cooked by boiling and steaming, and the dried skin toasted over the fire, while the dried white flesh was dipped in oil and eaten raw.

Cod and kelp fish were also taken with a line, anchored in a horizontal position near the bottom, to which a number of baited hooks were attached. Some of the Kwakiutl fastened the sinkers so that they were detached before the line was pulled up, saving the exertion of drawing them to the surface.

WOMEN PREPARING HALIBUT AT NEAH BAY

36

FISH HOOKS OF NORTHWEST COAST.

HARPOON FISHERMAN

SALMON TRAP FOR SMALL STREAM.

WEIR FOR TRAPPING EULACHON.

SALMON HARPOONS.

For many of the Northwest Coast tribes salmon supplied a large proportion of the food. They were formerly taken by a number of methods. Trolling was practised with a straight hook provided with a sharp barb placed at an acute angle. The baited hook trailed on the end of a line which the fisherman held in his hand as he paddled. The motion thus imparted to the hook simulated the movement of a live fish and attracted the salmon.

Where the condition of the water permitted, a two-pronged spear, similar to the one employed in harpooning porpoises, was employed. Long nets were formerly used by the Salish who lived near Victoria. Nets were woven from nettle fiber twine.

Nets were also used by the other tribes, especially in the rivers, where they were stretched between two canoes by means of which they were drawn down with the current or against the flow of the tide. These were either gill nets, in which the fish were caught when they tried to pass through, or they were provided with trailing pockets, into which the salmon passed.

The commonest method of taking salmon was by means of a weir across or at the sides of a stream, associated with which were fish baskets for collecting the fish or an advantageous place for spearing them. Because of the variations in the size, depth, and swiftness of the streams, there were many forms of these weirs and traps, adapted to the particular localities where they were used. The character of some of these will be readily observed in the illustrations.

In shallow rivers, such as the Nimkish in the Kwakiutl territory, and the Chilkat River of the Tlingit area, dog salmon were easily secured by means of a hook attached to a long pole. The hook was drawn along the bottom toward the canoe in which the fisherman stood. This method of fishing was pursued at night, unless the river was sufficiently roily, as is the case with the Chilkat River, so that the salmon do not see the fisherman. The fish themselves were so numerous that it was not necessary that the fishermen see them. Along the rivers were suitable places for fishing from a platform extending from the bank over a pool or eddy. The fisherman used either a net, a gaff hook, or a harpoon. Such favorable fishing sites were highly prized possessions.

The women received the salmon at the shore and prepared them for curing. The heads, tails, and fins were removed and the fish split down the back. The heads and tails were boiled or steamed and eaten fresh, while the sliced bodies and the roe were hung on poles to dry in the smoke of the fires.

SALMON BASKET TRAP.   DAM AND FISH TRAP.

COWICHAN RIVER FISH WEIR.

SALMON TRAP AT HAZELTON ON SKEENA RIVER.

COWICHAN RIVER FISH WEIR.

NOOTKA FISH TRAP.

FISH BASKETS.

HERRING EGGS DRYING. SITKA TLINGIT, 1889.

Another fish of great importance in the life of the northwestern people, was the eulachon. These fish are rather small, nine to twelve inches long, but they arrive at the mouths of certain rivers in great multitudes. The Nass River, in the Tsimshian country, is one of the best rivers for eulachon. The first arrivals are in the middle of March and the fish continue to run for about six weeks. As the fish come up to the mouth of the river, they are pursued by seals, sea-lions, and whales; and while in the river, great flocks of seagulls appear every day and feed upon them until night.

Piles were driven deep into the stream bed with stone pile drivers. Sliding on these posts were rings to which the net was attached. The lower rings were pushed to the bottom of the river with a pole when the net was open for use. The nets were long, bag-shaped, with wide mouths. While the ice from the upper river was running out, fishing was difficult, for the nets were liable to be carried away; and canoe navigation in the running ice was hazardous. After the ice had disappeared the nets had to be opened anew at every tide.

The oil from the fish used to be tried out by placing hot rocks in large wooden vessels, or canoes, thus keeping the water boiling until the oil from the fish gathered on the surface, where it was recovered after it cooled. After boiling, the fish were pressed, to force out the remaining oil. Formerly, the women accomplished this by squeezing the still hot fish against their naked breasts. The accumulations resulting from this process were not allowed to be wiped off until the season was over. Nowadays, the oil is rendered in home-made furnaces of sheet metal under which fires can be maintained and presses with levers are provided for extracting the oil. It was customary to allow the fish to decay somewhat before submitting them to this process, since the oil was then more easily separated, and the Indians are not prejudiced against the odor or taste of slightly putrid fish oil.

Eulachon oil was highly prized; dried salmon, halibut, and other foods were dipped into it and formed a favorite sauce for such dishes as dried berries and smoked meats. Trade in eulachon oil was formerly very extensive. Indians from a distance came to the favorable fishing places and bought temporary rights to fish and render the oil. Long trails, known as "grease trails," led into the interior, where the coast people traded with the Athaspascan-speaking tribes. The oil was carried by canoe and also traded among the Northwest Coast people. It does not deteriorate with time and may, therefore, be stored for a year or two. This was fortunate for great runs of eulachon do not occur every year.

The spawn of herring was collected for food, usually by anchoring quantities of cedar or hemlock brush in the spawning places. When the brush was withdrawn it was covered with a mass of eggs. The Tlingit and Tsimshian gathered the seaweed on which the herring spawned. The herring themselves were secured with a rake, a stick with a row of sharp pieces of bone set in one side; but in more recent times, nails replaced the bone spikes. The fisherman sat in the stern of the canoe while his wife paddled in the bow, driving the canoe astern. The rake was swung edgewise through the water, the fish being impaled on the points and shaken off into the canoe. Eulachon were also taken in this manner. In early spring, herring were driven to the coast in numbers so great that they could scarcely find room in the shallow water.

EULACHON IN PITS FOR OIL AND DRYING.

EULACHON DRYING.   KWAKIUTL

PIT OF EULACHON ROTTING FOR EXTRACTION OF OIL.

EULACHON DRYING ON NASS RIVER.

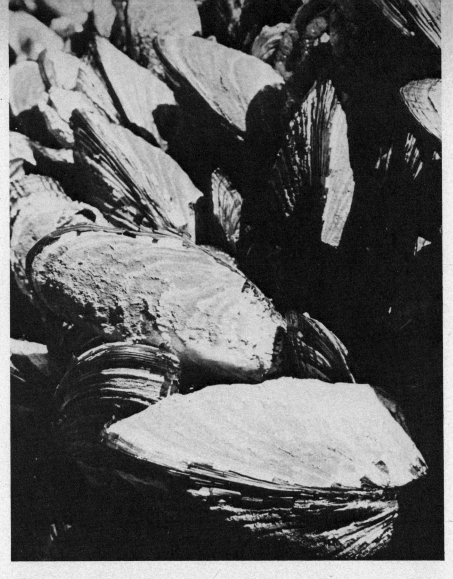

EDIBLE MUSSELS LINE OUTER COAST ROCKS.

ABUNDANCE OF LIFE ON THE BEACH.

DIGGING STICKS.

Shellfish. Beside these major products of the sea certain minor ones such as shellfish are of considerable importance.

The large horse clam was also used for food. The shells of these are eight or ten inches in length. They were secured with some difficulty, as the clams are capable of descending into the sand with considerable speed. These were cooked by steaming and because of their size were strung on three sticks. They were then exposed to fire and smoke as were the smaller clams. There are two important species of clams. The more common one is of ordinary size and fairly abundant. It was the woman's duty to dig them, in former times, with a digging-stick and a large shell. In transporting them she protected herself from the salt water, by placing a mat on her back under the carrying basket. For immediate use these clams were roasted over a fire, or steam-cooked in a box. When larger quantities were prepared for future use, they were steamed under a covering of seaweeds and mats. In this case, the clams were removed from the shells and strung on sticks or a strand of bark. These were exposed for some time to the heat of a fire and then smoked until they were thoroughly cured.

Cockles, mussels, crabs and horse clams and many other forms of sea life contributed to the food supply which was so abundant that famine was practically unknown among the tribes living directly on the coast.

Vegetables. The vegetable diet of the Indians of the Northwest Coast was quite varied, but not particularly abundant. They did not practise agriculture as did some of the Indians east of the Rocky Mountains in the United States, nor did they have acorns in abundance as in California. From the sea they took eelgrass and seaweed. They utilized fern and bracken, and camas roots. They had a fair variety of wild fruits including elderberries, huckleberries, salmon berries, gooseberries, rose hips, salal berries, and crab-apples. The roots were cooked by steaming in underground ovens or were roasted on the coals and eaten with oil. The seaweed was allowed to decay a little before being dried and stored for winter use. The dried weed was chopped up with an adze and chewed before being boiled and served in oil. The berries were usually cooked, dried, and stored in cakes for future use. These were soaked in water, broken up, kneaded until soft, covered with oil, and eaten with a spoon. Huckleberries were boiled with salmon spawn and packed in wooden boxes sealed with eulachon fat. Wild crab-apples served with oil were a favorite dish. Starches, except in the south, were poorly represented, and were found chiefly in the form of camas bulbs. In southern British Columbia and in Washington and Oregon the camas is plentiful. It was cooked in quantities in underground ovens and provided excellent and palatable food. In the spring quantities of the inner bark, cambium layer, of the hemlock were removed and stored for winter use.

The camas roots mentioned above were secured from low ground where a wild camas grows abundantly. These gardens were family property which could not be sold or given away, but descended in the family by inheritance. The camas roots were dug in the autumn after the leaves of the trees had fallen. Pebbles were removed and roots unsuitable for food were sometimes replanted, but otherwise the plots were not cultivated by the owner.

The cultivation of potatoes was introduced in the period of the early voyages by explorers and trades, and quickly spread wherever conditions were favorable.

WOMEN GATHERING SEAWEED.

BERRIES ADDED FOR VARIETY TO FISH MEALS.

WOMEN DIGGING ROOTS.

WOMEN RETURNING WITH FOOD.

43

BEAR IN DEAD FALL.

KWAKIUTL BOWS AND ARROWS.

SPRING TRAP USED FOR BEAR AND DEER.

Animals. As has been previously stated, the people of the Northwest Coast secured the greater part of their food supply from the ocean and only a minor portion by the hunting of land mammals. Deer were taken either in snares or shot with bow and arrow. The Nootka had certain restrictions regarding the eating of deer and fish during the same season. Bears killed in deadfalls were given a ceremonial welcome and feast. Eating bear meat also involved a taboo against salmon.

Mountain goats were frequently hunted by the mainland tribes. They did not occur on the islands. Nooses were set in the trails where there was a sheer wall above and below so that the trail must be used. The goats were also run with dogs and when cornered or brought to bay were taken by dropping a noose over their heads. The wool was much prized for the making of blankets. The flesh was eaten fresh or cured with smoke and in the sun, and stored away in large quantities for future use.

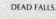

BIRD SPEAR.

DEAD FALLS.

BLACK BEAR WITH SPAWNED OUT SALMON.

MOUNTAIN GOAT.

COAST BLACKTAIL DEER.

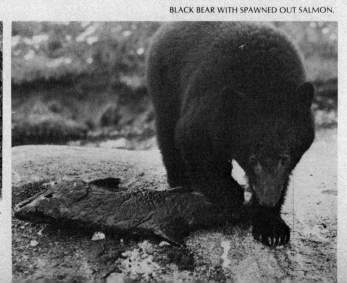

Dress and Decoration

The mild climate of the Northwest Coast made warm clothing unnecessary and the damp weather was a factor which militated against the use of skins for clothing. Consequently, we find the tribes of this area wearing a minimum amount of clothing. The men went about entirely nude during the summer months and the women wore only a grass skirt closely resembling that worn in Polynesia. Clothing was worn as a protection against rain rather than against cold. Leather garments are of small value in a wet climate and we find the tribes of this area employing instead clothing of vegetable fiber.

Footgear. One of the striking features of the Northwest Coast costume, distinguishing it from the remainder of North America, is the almost total lack of footwear. Except in the far north and in the interior, the Northwest Coast people were bare-legged and bare-footed, summer and winter. They were unaccustomed to extensive land travel and, therefore, needed less protection for their feet than did the Indians living inland. The cold months are also wet months and untanned leather soon became water-soaked and of doubtful value as foot covering.

Men's Clothing. The men of the Coast were accustomed to go about in summer entirely devoid of clothing. For ceremonial occasions and in winter a rectangular robe of skins or woven fiber was wrapped around the body under the left arm and over the right shoulder, hanging to the knees. When Europeans first visited the coast, many of these robes were made of sea-otter skin and their purchase from the backs of the people inaugurated the fur trade of that coast.

Waterproof mats, cut like a poncho, were worn by both men and women in wet weather.

The beard was eradicated, except by some of the older men; the hair was worn long, loose, or bunched on top of the head. Slaves were compelled to wear their hair short. Hats were worn only as a protection against the rain. On dress occasions especially, the body and face were coated with oil over which red ocher, mica, and sparkling sand were applied. On all religious occasions, white down was strewed over the hair. Down was a symbol of peace and goodwill and its use is often mentioned in the early accounts. The men were very fond of ear and nose pendants, using twigs of cedar, feathers, pieces of wood and bone, and, when they could be secured, metal objects of all descriptions.

BOW FISHERMAN.

MAN WITH SLAVE KILLER AROUND NECK.

STARTING FIRE.

45

THE REED GATHERER.

FOOD GATHERERS.

Women's Dress. The woman wore aprons of shredded bark tied around the waist and reaching the knees. Except on rare ceremonial occasions, this garment was not laid aside in public. Ordinarily, the women also wore a cedarbark garment which covered them from the shoulders, where it was fastened about the neck, to the ankles. A girdle was worn with this, confining the garment to the waist; they also wore tight bands about the ankles, as well as bracelets, nose, and earrings. In the north, the Tsimshian, Haida, and Tlingit women slit their lower lips and inserted a wooden plug. This opening was increased in size according to her age and rank so that the lip plug or labret of grooved wood might ultimately measure three by four inches. This held her lip in a horizontal position as long as she wore it; otherwise the lip drooped down on her chin.

Deformed Heads. Two types of head deformation were practised on the Pacific Coast. In Washington and northward among the related Salish of British Columbia, the forehead was flattened so that the head sloped back from the eyes to a summit at the back. Since this treatment was not permitted for the slaves, an undeformed head indicated a freeman. Just north of the area where head flattening was practised, another style prevailed among the Kwakiutl. The top of the head was bound so as to decrease its diameter and elongate it upward and backward.

NOOTKA HAT.

TLINGIT COSTUMES.

KWAKIUTL WOMAN'S APRON.

HAIDA WOMAN WEARING LABRET

DENTALIUM SHELL ORNAMENTS

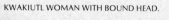

KWAKIUTL WOMAN WITH BOUND HEAD.

HAIR ORNAMENTS OF DETALIUM SHELLS.

KWAKIUTL WOMEN WITH DEFORMED HEADS

SOCIAL AND POLITICAL ORGANIZATION

Social Distinctions

In preceding sections there has been repeated mention of such groups as the Haida, Tlingit, Kwakiutl, etc. Actually, these are not single tribes, but linguistic groups, each of which consists of a number of tribes which are further divided into sub-tribes. Each of these sub-tribes may, in turn, consist of a number of village groups. Actually, it was these village groups which were the basic social units of the Northwest Coast people.

In addition, the Tlingit, Haida, and Tsimshian had certain artificial social divisions, membership in which depended upon descent through the mother. These groups were known as clans, and one belonged to the same clan as his mother. Among the Kwakiutl groups, the Bella Coola, and certain other tribes, there was a curious division into septs. South of the Kwakiutl the tribes were simply organized on the basis of village groups.

The Indians of the Northwest Coast differ from the other natives of North America in the amount of emphasis they place upon wealth and property and upon the ceremonial distribution of wealth. Closely linked with this was the concept of an aristocracy of blood. In each village group there tended to be one to several families of wealth and distinction and of aristocratic blood who consequently dominated within the village in which they resided. Below this "nobility" of wealth and lineage was a second group of persons less wealthy or less closely related to the dominating families; they were the poor relations of the nobility, the general run of the population. Below these was the third and last class, the slaves. These were captives taken in war or such captives purchased from other tribes together with their descendants.

To be rich meant to be well born and conversely to be well born usually meant that a man was wealthy. Wealth was not held so much for wealth's sake, but rather its possession enabled a man to show the greatness of his family. This he did by making ceremonial distributions of this wealth at stated intervals or for certain occasions. In this way he exhalted the honor of his family and indicated his wealth was so great that he could distribute or destroy it with impunity.

Below the wealthy chiefs the social classes graded downward without formal rankings. First, were those closely related to the high born chiefs; below these, others less closely related; and further down the scale, the poor relations of the chiefs who were usually hangers-on at their households. There was also a rather illy-defined middle class who, while not of high birth, possessed some worldly goods. It was sometimes possible for a member of this class to rise

HORNED OWL DESIGN ON COPPER.

CHIEF WITH COPPER.

SLAVE-KILLERS

somewhat in the social scale through the accumulation of wealth. Usually this made it possible for a man to marry a child into a family of higher rank, thereby raising himself in the esteem of his fellow tribesmen. Below this median stratum, and at the bottom of the social scale, were the slaves. Slavery was known among nearly all of the tribes of North America, but the slaves were usually war captives who were adopted into the tribe and consequently suffered few if any social disabilities. However, on the Northwest Coast where there was so strong a development of a sense of aristocracy and wealth, slaves were held as mere chattels and both they and their descendants remained slaves and were regarded as being merely a form of property to be traded, given away, or killed, to enhance the prestige of their masters. A slave or a descendant of a slave could not rise above his social class.

Septs. Over the greater part of the Northwest Coast there were groups of considerable size, the members of which considered themselves related at least to the extent of being descended from the same "first ancestors." Thus, they might be likened to the several branches of a family line. These extended families, or septs, were distinguished by names which served as do our surnames in holding their members together. Theoretically, all chiefs were merely heads of such extended families, but the chiefs differed in rank so that the head of the family of the highest rank in the sept, was chief of the sept. The chief of the sept ranking the highest in the village was the chief of the village.

Just as there were varying but definite gradations of rank among the common people, so the chiefs were definitely graded. Among the Kwakiutl this grading of the chiefs was mainly, or perhaps entirely on the theory of primogeniture. The oldest son was the head of the house; the oldest son in the line of the oldest sons in the sept, village, and group held the headship in each. This was not necessarily the real origin of the order of rank, but the Kwakiutl were accustomed to interpret social distinctions in this manner. In this estimate of worth and standing, the mother as well as the father was considered; therefore, a chief strove to marry as high in rank as possible and thereby elevated the position of his descendants. If he married beneath his rank he lowered the position of his family and such a blot was remembered from generation to generation. In reality, this may have been the native way of explaining that certain families were less highly esteemed than others.

Chiefs. As has been stated, at the top of the social pyramid were the chiefs and those so close to them that they had a kind of reflected glory. In principle, the chief differed only in degree from the lesser individuals. Like them, he inherited a named house, together with the right to decorate it with certain carvings and paintings; a number of feast dishes with names for them, as well as names for his canoes; certain traditional names for himself and the members of his family; family origin myths which were publicly dramatized; and other dignities. In addition, he inherited the duty of controlling the social unit of which he was the head.

Rivalry of Chiefs. While it is probable that the relative order of ranking for the chiefs was stable from generation to generation, constant attempts were made by them to increase their prestige at the expense of their rivals. In this rivalry, they resorted to methods similar to those employed by the common people to secure their advancement. In connection with the same events in family life, birth, puberty, marriage, and death, the chiefs distributed property and gave feasts, and carried them out on a still greater scale. In addition to these general ceremonies, the chiefs sought opportunities for outdoing their rivals and putting them to shame. One form of rivalry among the Kwakiutl was to give an "oil feast" during which the eulachon oil was served with other food and great quantities of the precious fluid were thrown upon the fire, or allowed to flow on to it from above. The flames leapt up and often set the roof of the house on fire. The guest, who was the rival, had to retain his seat near the fire, keeping his composure until the host gave the order to abate the flames, and extinguish the fire which was burning the house above them. However, if the guest believed that he had not been outdone; that at some time he himself had given a greater feast, he was privileged to refuse to accept the proffered spoon of oil and went to his house to bring a "copper" which he broke and gave to his host, and thus "put out the fire." Not to be outdone, the host, in his absence, had to attach a copper to each of the four house posts. If beaten, the guest was "shamed," and soon was under obligation to give a greater feast to remove the smirch of his reputation.

SEA-GRIZZLY BEAR CREST

DOGFISH CREST

Another form of rivalry consisted in breaking up coppers. The coppers were shield-shaped with a rib running across the middle and from the center to one end. They were of native manufacture, the older ones being made of metal found in a free state near Copper River. Each had a name and a well-known history and its value depended on this history and the amount for which it had been sold. One chief broke a copper of well-known value and gave the pieces to his rival who was compelled to destroy a copper of equal or greater value and give in return the parts of both, or lose in prestige. A more extreme act was to break a copper and throw the parts into the sea. Canoes were also sunk and slaves killed.

These property contests generally occurred between chiefs who were traditional rivals. They may have been chiefs of septs or of villages, or the leaders of more remote groups. In all of these contests the chief acted for the members of his group who contributed very largely to the property used. It is certain also that for some of the peoples of the Northwest Coast the chief had a symbolic relation to his group, so that there was an emotional transfer to him of its power and prestige. If he succeeded in raising his rank, he carried the group up with him. If he suffered insult, the group was correspondingly put to shame.

Feasts. In addition to serving as a weapon in social rivalry, accumulated wealth was also distributed in more purely social feasts. Practically every social event required the giving of a feast which in turn necessitated a proper house and an ample supply of food. Every such event also required the distribution of property, some of it was in payment for services rendered, but much of it was bestowed on the guests of the occasion, according to their rank. The events requiring feasts were the naming of a child; the puberty of girls and at that time the piercing of the ears, and nose, and the lower lip for the labret; the tattooing of both sexes; the burial of a relative; the building of a house; and the assumption of a predecessor's position and rank. The relative importance of the events varied according to the tribe. The Nootka placed the puberty ceremony first while the Tlingit and Haida held in highest esteem the ceremony attending the final placing of the remains of a deceased relative. Whenever one of these events occurred, the person who gave the ceremony assumed a new name, and displayed by carvings, paintings, or, more generally, by dramatic representation, one or more of his inherited honors.

A man's renown was increased according to the frequency of the celebrations and the lavishness with which they were carried out. In order to give them at all, he must have inherited or acquired certain names and honors which he could publicly assume or display. The inherited names or honors came from his father's or mother's line, according to the tribal rules of inheritance. Among the Nootka they were inherited from either father or mother, with the Kwakiutl some of them always descended from the father to the eldest child; among the Bella Coola they were willed, according to a fixed rule; while among the northern tribes the more important ones passed from a man to his sister's son. Names and honors or crests particularly among the Kwakiutl were secured through marriage. The father-in-law bestowed these upon his son-in-law, who in turn passed them on to his son-in-law, thus only property received in marriage was bestowed through marriage. A man greedy for honors endeavored to marry well and often. It was not necessary in every case actually to take the woman in order to acquire the honors. In fact, if there were no daughter, a man might go through the form of marriage with a man's foot in order to perpetuate names and honors.

Not only was it necessary that a certain number of inherited names or honors be acquired through marriage in order that these socially elevating ceremonies may be held; but the opportunities to acquire wealth had to exist. Hunting and fishing grounds were the chief possessions. Generally, also, slaves and dependent relatives were required to assist the accumulation of property. Also a great deal was added by skill and application. Canoes were excellent forms of property acquired through skill and labor alone. In early times, successful hunting resulted in the possession of furs and skins which were directly distributed; more recently, these were, of course, readily exchanged for woolen blankets which became the units of exchange.

A certain element of the population thus acquired fortune through birth and another through personal ability and activity. The inherited names were of little value unless the second element were added. Inherited names were only potential honors until assumed with lavish feasting and a distribution of wealth. But through personal achievement a man might greatly elevate his position during his life, and might bring about advancement for his descendants. Because of the social obligation to distribute this wealth, constant efforts had to be made to produce new assets. By including neighboring tribes in ceremonies of this sort it was possible to extend one's fame beyond the tribe. When a position had been acquired, it received constant public recognition, since a guest's name was proclaimed as he entered a house, and a seat assigned to him according to his rank.

Inherited Duties. There were many inherited public duties which brought the recipient no special renown. Among these, especially for the Kwakiutl, may be enumerated the public accounting of property. These public accountants were able to list the amount of property out on loan at any time; they were tally keepers, who counted and tallied blankets and other property when publicly transferred. There were also singers who improvised and taught songs to those initiated in certain societies. Among the Bella Coola one man inherited the duty of enforcing the taboos and regulations in regard to the river. Many specific duties related to feasts and the taking or preparation of the first fish or fruits of the season.

Exogamous Divisions. In addition to the grouping according to tribe, sept, and village, some of the tribes of this area had another type of social grouping, that according to a rule of unilateral descent. Every member of the tribe was by birth a member of one of these formal divisions and by rule belonged to the same group as his mother. This kind of social grouping is found in other parts of America and elsewhere and is designated as a clan or a sib system. As is nearly always the case, these groups regulated marriage, that is, a man must marry a woman from outside his own clan.

In order to understand the clan systems two essential points must be observed, first, that descent is recorded either on the father's (paternal) or the mother's (maternal) side; second, that all the members of one's group are counted as relatives, and none of them can

EAGLE CREST

KILLER WHALE CREST

KWAKIUTL GIRL

be considered as a mate in marriage. On the Northwest Coast this type of organization was known among all of the tribes of the Tsimshian, Tlingit, and Haida. Among the Tlingit and Haida and the Nass River Tsimshian there were two such groups, while among the other Tsimshian tribes there were four. The Haida groups were called Eagle and Raven; those of the Tlingit and Nass River Tsimshian, Raven and Wolf; the Tsimshian proper and the Gitksan Tsimshian were grouped into Raven, Eagle, Wolf, and Bear. Because a man and his wife were necessarily members of different clans this divided the family as well as the tribe. In addition to regulating marriage these groups had certain religious, social, and political functions.

The Haida were divided into two groups or clans, one called Ravens and the other Eagles. This division affected the whole tribe, because it runs also through every family. If the husband were a Raven his wife and children were Eagles; if the husband were an Eagle his wife and children were Ravens. Since, as has been stated above, such social grouping, is a well-recognized and widely distributed phenomenon, there is no reason to look for an origin of such groups in geographical distribution, or migration. The two essentials of such groups have been mentioned above; namely, descent in one line only, and an imputed relationship preventing marriage. In addition, there may be religious, social, and political distinctions as well. Among the Haida, the rank, names, ceremonial duties and properties, fishing rights, and house of a man had to remain in his own division. Since his children belonged to the opposite division, he chose for his heir, his sister's son; and in order that the sister's son might become familiar with the duties and properties he was to inherit, he lived with his uncle as soon as he was old enough to leave his mother. In case of violent quarrels between members of the two divisions a man's wife and sons adhered to their own clan and aligned themselves with his enemies, to whom they might even be expected to betray him.

The ceremonial connection of the Haida divisions was with burial and the accompanying rites. The body was prepared and buried by the father's family, members of the opposite division, which was recompensed by a potlatch. The division had no direct political functions since these pertain rather to the various families or septs. Since every sept belonged to either one of the divisions, and all the members of a sept were members of the same division, it was true that members of the same sept might not marry.

The Kwakiutl Bella Bella had four divisions in the north and five in the south; these were not marriage regulating, but merely local and social groups. They were equated, however, with the corresponding divisions of their northern neighbors and may be regarded as an attempt to imitate the social organization of the north.

In the south, the Salish counted descent and inherited, as we do, in both the father's and the mother's line. Usually a man sought a wife in some other village and brought her to his own village to live. A man's son was his usual heir, but a man also inherited honors and property from his mother's people, as well as from his father.

Among the Kwakiutl it is thought that a method originally similar to that of the Salish has been influenced from the north. The names and positions of the heads of various septs and families were inherited by the oldest son or daughter and their descendants. There were, however, many names carrying social and ceremonial positions, which were transmitted by a man through his son-in-law to his daughter's child. A child, other than the first born, may belong to his father's or his mother's sept (*numaym*) according to the parents' wishes. Whether a child was assigned to his father's or his mother's *numaym* usually depended upon the relative rank of the father and mother, and the privileges at their disposal. It was also a common practice, for a dying person to bestow his position by an expressed wish which was followed, if it were not too contrary to the established social customs. In certain of the noble Kwakiutl families an attempt was made to retain the privilege within the family by close intermarriage, such as between half brothers and sisters, or marriage of a man with his younger brother's daughter.

The Bella Coola do not have such clearly marked divisions; and, in order to strengthen the family power and prestige, were much given to close intermarriage. Marriage between cousins or the children of cousins was not approved, but a union between the grandchildren of cousins was regarded as ideal. It may be added that even among the northern tribes, where the divisions existed, the noble families intermarried, generation after generation, but always on the father's side.

YOUNG CLAYOQUOT GIRL

Puberty

As among most primitive people the world over, the tribes of the Northwest Coast gave social and ceremonial recognition to the period of adolescence. At the time of puberty the girls of the Northwest Coast were, for a period, secluded, restricted as to their diet and movements, and observed special taboos. Even in the same tribe, there was considerable variation in detail as to these observances.

However, there was general agreement among the Northwest Coast tribes in placing the girl behind a screen; in requiring her to abstain from all food and drink for some days, and from certain foods for one or several years; and in guarding hunting, fishing, and gambling equipment, as well as fish and fish streams from her. Two kinds of reasons were assigned for these practices: First, that the girl herself would be influenced by conformity, or lack of conformity with these regulations. Whatever happened to her at this time would affect her throughout her life; second, that her actions would have an effect on other persons and on things. A hunter, meeting her, would lose his luck; salmon would fail to run if she saw them, or if she crossed the stream; should she look at a running dog it would be stopped by her glance. These reasons may be conceived of in part, as inventions to frighten the girl into obedience. Behind some of them, no doubt, lay the belief that the girl, during this time, was endowed with great supernatural or magical power. Among the Nootka the coming of age of a daughter was an occasion for giving a potlatch of special grandeur.

DOUBLE COLUMNED MORTUARY, SKEDANS, Q.C.Is.

Burial Customs

Tree Burial. The Nootka and the southern Kwakiutl formerly resorted chiefly to tree burial. The bodies were folded and placed in large boxes which were carried into the tall timber and placed high up in a tree. Care was taken to select a tree rendered inaccessible because it leaned out over a chasm or over water; all the limbs below the body were also cut away so that climbing the tree thereafter would be difficult. The place chosen was some distance from the village, often on an island. Bodies were also placed in caves, provided suitable ones were available. Among the Nootka, the burial caves belonged to the more important families. The Kwakiutl viewed burial in the earth with considerable horror when contact with Europeans first brought the custom to their notice, but they have now adopted the practice.

Canoe Burial. The Salish tribes of Washington often used canoes as receptacles for the dead and their belongings. These were elevated on scaffolds or placed in trees beyond the reach of animals.

Cremation. The Tsimshian burned the dead except for the heart, which was removed and buried. With shamans, however, the internal organs were buried, and the body placed in a grave house above ground. The Haida and Tlingit also burned all but the shamans whom they placed in grave houses in some isolated place. The bones, after the cremation, were gathered together and placed in elevated boxes or in mortuary columns.

The intimate personal belongings of the deceased were burned, or, in more recent times, placed near the grave.

NOOTKA BURIAL CAVE

TLINGIT GRAVE HOUSES

Memorial Columns. It was the practice of all of the tribes to erect a monument near the burial place of the more prominent dead. Usually this consisted of a wooden carving representing the principal crests of the deceased. Recently, similar carvings made in stone have been substituted for wooden ones. Burial among the northern tribes was always carried out by the members of the clan or division of which the deceased was not a member — that is by the members of his father's division. Among the Tlingit and Haida, those who buried a man were necessarily members of his wife's clan. It was the rule among the Kwakiutl to have people unrelated to them cut the hair of the mourners. The performance of such duties involved payment, which was accomplished in public and with a feast; that is to say, it was a potlatch occasion. Among the Tlingit it was the main occasion for giving a potlatch and took place when the remains were placed in their final resting place, and the mortuary column was erected. Because the work was by the opposite clan, they were the recipients of the distributed property.

SALISH GRAVE NEAR LYTTON

SINGLE AND. . .

DOUBLE COLUMN MORTUARIES

HORIZONTAL MEMORIAL FIGURE

Marriage

Selection of Mates. The choice of a mate was subject to restrictions varying according to the tribal customs and the social standing of the individuals concerned. Among all the tribes, it was almost indispensable that marriage should be between equals in rank. While this was the ideal, some accommodation to the supply and demand of mates was permitted; especially where the tribal population was small. In the south, among the Nootka and Salish, near relatives were avoided, whether on the father's or the mother's side. There was a tendency, moreover, among the Salish to marry outside the village. In the north, the Haida and Tlingit were divided into two exogamous matrilineal groups; therefore, and since a man always belonged to his mother's group, he must always select a mate from his father's group. The Tsimshian, being divided into four groups, were not compelled to marry into the father's clan.

The Kwakiutl of Vancouver Island and the neighboring mainland emphasized kinship in the father's sept and married into some other. There was, however, a counter tendency, especially in the families of higher rank, to intermarry in order to retain the crests and privileges within the sept.

The Bella Coola had neither matrilineal clans, nor exogamous regulations. On the other hand, intermarriage between certain families was customary in order to concentrate social possessions and social position, rather than suffer their dispersion through marriage with outsiders. Since rights and honors, in addition to those inherited, were mainly obtainable through marriage, a father eager to improve the position of his descendants will marry his daughter to several men in succession, even before she reaches puberty. The honors so accumulated passed on to his grandchildren, regardless of which particular man was their parent. Marriage between cousins or children of cousins was not allowed, but the most favored marriage was between grandchildren of cousins. Intermarriage between certain related families continued for generations.

While, as stated before, the northern tribes always avoided the mother's group there was no such regulation in regard to the father's relatives. The conventional marriage for a Tsimshian youth was with his mother's younger brother's daughter. The rule that only those equal in rank should mate, greatly reduced the choice of the few families of high station so that constant intermarriage on the father's side became necessary. It was formerly the custom for the head chiefs of two of the more important Tsimshian tribes to marry each other's sister, generation after generation. So complicated were the various social conditions among the Tlingit, that the choice of a mate for a member of the higher aristocracy, was sometimes reduced to two or three individuals.

Equality in age was not given much consideration. Among the northern tribes, where the sister's son succeeded his uncle, inheriting property and privileges from him, he was expected to marry his uncle's widow. When he became older, however, there was an opportunity to secure a bride much younger than himself. Such inequalities of age were regarded with favor.

Marriage Customs. There was considerable uniformity throughout the area in the method of carrying out marriages. Everywhere it was the custom for a family to reside in the village of the husband. The general custom seemed to have been for the bridegroom's relatives to approach the bride's family formally, with presents or promises of presents. A certain degree of hesitation was ordinarily shown by the bride's family, which took the form, as it did with the Salish in the south, of keeping the bridegroom waiting and fasting for some days. The Nootka and Kwakiutl had certain ordeals peculiar to each particular family, which had to be passed successfully by the groom, or by his representatives. One such ordeal was to compel the bridegroom to pass by a very hot fire. There was often also some bickering over the value of the presents offered; not of a mercenary character, but to emphasize the high standing of the parties concerned. The acceptance of the presents by the bride's family was followed by return gifts of equal or greater value. By the Salish these were delivered within a few days to the village of the bridegroom where the bride was taken to reside.

Among the Kwakiutl, the bride's father announced, at the time of the wedding, that he would give his son-in-law certain property and honors. These were usually not delivered until a child was born to the couple, and often, not until the child was old enough to be initiated into the ceremonies. The amount given by the bride's father was sometimes five times that received from the bridegroom, but this varied according to the number and sex of the children. The Kwakiutl considered that this payment dissolved the marriage. The wife, if she were the first one, ordinarily continued to live with her husband, but with a greater degree of independence since she was free to return to her home if she wished. If her husband were ambitious for honors and able to pay for them, he made presents again to his father-in-law, renewing his marriage. In due time he received in return more than he had given in property, as well as additional names and honors. In all these cases the transfer of property took place at a public gathering where the witnesses were feasted. Since the property thus received was distributed to the husband's sept within a day or two, the son-in-law benefitted, not in property, but only in the new and higher honors which he had received. However, in all ordinary cases, he transferred these to his son, or his daughter's husband, in the same manner as he himself had received them.

The Haida mother often made an engagement for her son or daughter while they were still quite young and ensured its validity by a present of blankets. The family of the boy took the initiative among the Masset and the family of the girl among the Skidegate. When the ceremony occurred, the speeches made by the boy's relatives praised the girl and her family, while her own spokesmen belittled her and her abilities. This procedure was the reverse of that among the Nootka, where each party bestowed praises on his own family.

STONE DAGGERS

COPPER AND STEEL DAGGERS

Games

The Northwest Coast people were quite addicted to gambling. The most popular game was the well-known and widely distributed one of guessing by the expression of the opponent's face where a marked stick was concealed. The objects necessary were a number of sets of sticks about three-eighths of an inch in diameter and five inches long. The sticks of the same set were painted with the same pattern except the "ace" which was unmarked. Each set had a bag and a larger one held the various sets of the owner. The sets of sticks were laid out on a piece of skin, the playing was on a mat, the sticks were displayed on a second piece of hide while the guess was made. The opponents sat facing each other. The first player selected one of his sets of sticks, wrapped them in cedarbark, and divided them into two bundles which he placed before himself. His opponent then attempted to guess, by a study of the player's expression, in which bundle the "ace" was concealed. If he guessed correctly, he took the play, but if not, the former player continued. When one side attained a count of seven, four bundles were made instead of two; the player won the final point only if the guesser missed it after three trials. Such odds greatly prolonged the game. This game varied as to the objects used, but the main point, that of guessing from the opponent's expression and reactions was the same.

There were, in addition, dice games, shooting at a mark, a form of quoits, shinney, wrestling, and numerous other games. The stones used in the latter game were frequently found near the village sites. The Northwest Coast people, in common with those all over the world, had string figures or cat's cradles.

Warfare

While many of the winter villages were located with a view to comfortable living rather than defense, certain other village sites were chosen with an evident desire for security from attack. Ordinarily, a point of land was occupied so that the only approach was by a narrow passageway which could be cut off by means of ditches and stockades. In most instances these forts could be reduced by a few days' siege, for the Indians were not accustomed to long continued and tenacious fighting.

The two chief occasions for fighting were: revenge, and the securing of slaves. The feeling for a just balance, a life for a life, or an injury for an injury, was strongly developed and was active between families, villages, and larger groups. In several respects the Indians' views of such matters were quite unlike our own. In recent times, we have come to feel that retaliation for death or injury should fall upon the guilty individuals, but the Indians were as well satisfied if they took revenge on any member of the same group, or a person living in the same region. An example of this may be seen in a recorded account of the Kwakiutl. A canoe with its passengers, one of whom was a chief, failed to return from Victoria. Evidence pointed to indulgences in liquor and the resulting inability to navigate the boat properly. A war party went to the vicinity of Victoria and while they slept killed the first group of Indians found in that region. The motive was rather clearly shown to be the satisfaction afforded the living relatives and some assumed benefits thought to accrue to the souls of those who have met a violent death.

As might be expected, where rank was so important as on the Pacific Coast, a life for a life was not always satisfactory. When a man had been killed in a village, the Tlingit were said to have conferred as to his worth and then to have chosen as the object of their retaliation a man of equal value in the offending group. He was publicly called upon to come forth and be killed. The man actually guilty, being of too little worth to satisfy justice, escaped, or settled matters with the family of the man slain in his stead.

From the accounts available it appears that the usual method of waging war was as follows: The proposal for a war expedition was made in a public assembly by some man of influence. It was then determined whether other groups should be invited to cooperate with them, and a time was set for the expedition to leave. The warriors and their wives underwent purification; in the south, at least, this consisted of frequent bathing followed by scrubbing with boughs, fasting, and continence. The canoes were raised, scorched, and freshly rubbed on the outside. Certain religious and magical acts were performed to secure good luck. The wives were required to follow established rules of conduct in order to bring good fortune to the party. Travel was always by canoe; the crews were organized; with each was a man provided with kindlings for setting fire to houses, one with ropes for securing slaves, and guards to watch the canoes. Due care was exercised that information should not reach the enemy. The arrival was timed for the evening and the attack for the morning, at about dawn, that the victims might be caught asleep. At dusk a small scouting canoe was sent out. The exact number and position of the houses was noted and the attack planned accordingly, each canoe crew being assigned to a definite house. If revenge were the motive, men and women would be killed, but if the expedition were to secure slaves, unnecessary slaughter, especially of women, was avoided.

WHALE-RIB WAR CLUB

JADE-BLADED WAR CLUB.   TLINGIT

TLINGIT ARMOR

RELIGION AND CEREMONIAL LIFE

In dealing with so difficult a subject as religion it is well to take up various aspects in detail. One profitable division of the subject is into the beliefs concerning the universe on one hand, and on the other, the specific acts and general conduct which seem to have religious motives. On analysis the elaborate ceremonies of the Northwest Coast, which at first might be assumed to be mainly religious in character, prove to be largely dramatic, with the social and artistic features fully as prominent as the religious aspects.

Religious Beliefs. Religious beliefs were concerned with the past, the present, and the future. Beliefs regarding the past and the origin of the world were largely speculative and were generally formulated in myths which did not necessarily have much connection with human conduct. Those dealing with the future were also speculative and related particularly to the persistence of personality after death. The concept of the supernatural world was, however, of the greatest importance, since it very greatly influenced daily life.

There is no evidence that a belief in a supreme being was general, but among the Haida and the Bella Coola, it appears that such a definite conception did exist.

Haida Deities. The Haida refer to the supreme being as the Power of the Shining Heavens. They believed that human beings had no direct personal relations with this being, who is conceived of as the source from which all the other minor supernatural beings derived their power. It was with these secondary deities that man dealt. There were houses believed to be suspended from the sky, in one of which dwelt Wigit who kept account of all human beings, and, who when a baby was about to be born, reached behind himself and pulled out a stick, the length of which regulated the duration of the child's life.

Of the supernatural beings on the earth, the Creek-women were of great importance. Each stream was believed to have a female divinity whose abode was at the source of the river. She controlled the stream and all the fish in it. Another Creek-woman, Djilagons by name, was also an important mythological character. Underneath the Queen Charlotte Islands which constitute the Haida world stood "the sacred one standing and moving." His infrequent movements produced the earthquakes. Thunderbird was responsible for lightning and thunder.

In addition to these beings which from our point of view are purely imaginary, the Haida considered that practically all fish, birds, and land and sea mammals were similar to human beings, but possessed of varying degrees of supernatural power. All of them were capable of taking human form; or better, they possessed a human form, and

NOOTKA POLE

HAIDA HOUSE FRONTAL

assumed their other forms when consorting with men. Of all living things, the killer-whales were the greatest. They were believed to live in villages under the sea, usually near some point of land. These under-sea villages were definitely located and named. The body of the killer-whale was nothing but the canoe in which he was accustomed to travel. There were also salmon people, herring people, and on land, grizzly bear people, land-otter people, etc. It was not always clear whether the supernatural land-otter people, for instance, were or were not distinct from the animal. Probably there was much confusion in the native mind on this subject. It is important, however, to keep in mind that the Indian attitude toward animals was extremely different from our own. In Northwest Coast mythology are frequent references to a time when the animals were men, gifted with the power of speech and other human attributes. The people of the Northwest Coast believed that animals have souls which are immortal and that they are re-born after death. They are considered practically the equals of man in general intelligence, and to surpass him in the particulars for which the animal in question is especially noted.

Among the Haida, these animals were also divided into two sections: Ravens and Eagles corresponding to their two social groups. The killer-whales are differently marked so they can be distinguished; the Eagles have a white patch at the base of the dorsal fin. Many of the taboos and customs observed in hunting and fishing were adjustments to bring about social harmony between men and the "other peoples" used for food. One needs to realize that these were not, to the Indian's way of thinking, mythological beings, but real beings upon whose good will they were dependent.

Gods of the Kwakiutl. The Kwakiutl, like the Bella Coola, believed that the supernatural ones lived in houses, but unlike the Bella Coola, the Kwakiutl made the mysterious, heavily forested inland region, rather than the upper world, the home of these supernatural beings. Most frequently mentioned was the house in the north where lived the cannibal spirit who gave the Kwakiutl their most prized ceremony, and who was still believed to initiate all the candidates received into the Cannibal Society. Of more general religious significance was another house from which a different type of winter ceremony was derived. Incidentally, it appears that in this house the souls of all the plants, and perhaps also the smaller animals dwell. Since one of the performances held in this house was that of giving birth, it was probably believed that from this house all generation of men, animals, and plants, took place. In addition to these two houses somewhere on land there was one under the sea belonging to the killer-whales who are the greatest hunters of sea life. The Kwakiutl like the Haida considered all animals as potentially human-like and capable of assuming the appearance of men. The mountain goats, like the killer-whales, had a house in which they lived, as men do. Even the one domesticated animal, the dog, might assume a human form.

It is clear that the dominating religious concept was that bodies of men, animals, and plants, were the houses, canoes, or shells in which souls dwelt and that these souls had a great range of action outside of the habitations in which they were ordinarily found. The following Tsimshian myth will illustrate the attitude of the people toward the "salmon people."

A young prince was scolded by his mother for taking a certain dry salmon to give to his hungry slave. The prince was grieved and went down near the river. A canoe came, he entered, and was taken far out to sea. He arrived at a village where the carvings on the houses indicated that they belonged to Spring Salmon. The chief had been ill because the prince's mother had kept the dry salmon for two years and that particular salmon was his body. The slave's eating it had in some measure aided his recovery and, out of gratitude, he had sent for the prince. Whenever the prince was hungry he was instructed to club one of the children playing outside. The child immediately became a spring salmon. The prince was charged to put in the fire all the bones left after his meal. If this were done to the bones of the salmon, they would come to life again in their own country. Dry salmon must not be kept beyond the next season, for otherwise they are not released by being eaten and by the burning of their bones. When once the prince overlooked an eye, a child complained that one of his eyes hurt. As soon as the prince found the missing eye and burned it, the child's eye was well again.

TLINGIT SHAMAN AND HIS TWO WIVES

In spring the salmon chief, now fully recovered, sent scouts to the Skeena and Nass rivers to see if the cottonwood leaves were floating on the river. As soon as they were found, a journey was made to all the villages of the salmon people, and they were notified. Each variety of salmon had its own village from which the canoes set out in proper succession to go to the rivers where they appeared to the fishermen in their fish form. The chief of the spring salmon went to the shaman's net. After his names had been called over him he was cut open and was used in a feast from which all who were ceremonially unclean were excluded. All his bones were put in the fire and those who had eaten took a drink of fresh water. The prince was found in this chief salmon's stomach and rapidly grew to his former size. He instructed the people as to the things which must be observed in regard to salmon and finally returned to live with the salmon people.

Such concepts of an animal world, closely interrelated with the world of human beings, furnish much of the religious life and emotional atmosphere of the Northwest Coast.

TSIMSHIAN SHAMAN WORKING OVER SICK BOY

Religious Practices

Ceremonial Purity. In response to the religious ideas outlined in the last section, certain efforts were made to keep on good terms with the supernatural beings. Many rituals were performed in order to achieve ceremonial cleanliness. The supernatural beings were supposed to be very sensitive to odors. In part, this may be an entirely natural and practical observation in so far as it concerns game animals. Cleanliness was achieved by ritualistic bathing. For certain ceremonial occasions the baths were in the sea, but the most beneficial were in freshwater lakes. After the bath, the body was scrubbed with hemlock branches, often until the blood ran. Such baths were taken night and morning for four days or in four different

HAIDA CEREMONIAL SHIRTS

lakes. A man undertaking ceremonial duties was obliged to practise continence for days and sometimes weeks in advance. Women, unless well past middle age, were always of doubtful cleanliness, and were sometimes excluded from ceremonies as a matter of precaution. Abstention from food and water was believed to contribute greatly to an acceptable condition and for the same purpose the stomach was emptied by emetics.

Offerings. Food offerings, especially fat, were made. For water beings, the offerings were dropped into the sea, but for most other beings the gifts were placed in the fire. These offerings were not of any considerable bulk or value and do not seem to have been made with an idea of purchasing favors or goodwill. They were, rather, forms of social politeness.

Taboos. Many taboos had to be observed for fear of evil results. Naturally, many of these were concerned with salmon and fishing. Among the Tsimshian only mussel shells could be used for cutting salmon and among all the tribes metals were at first thought to be offensive. Mackenzie and other early travelers found it difficult to buy fresh salmon, the Indians fearing the fish would be cut with metal knives and cooked in metal dishes since it was believed that breaking of a taboo would "shame" the salmon and they would cease to run up the rivers.

The first salmon taken each year received special treatment. The Bella Coola placed it on a mat with its head on a pillow and offered it a piece of cedarbark. Afterward, eagle down was strewn over it and it was carried to the house and roasted. The Kwakiutl prayed to the first salmon caught each year and ate them immediately in a feast to which the men of the sept were invited.

The Nootka were accustomed to bring a bear which had been killed into the house, place it in a sitting position, put a hat on it, and sprinkle it with eagle down. The bear was offered food and invited to eat. The Tlingit also carried the grizzly bear's head into the house and decorated it with paint and eagle down.

SHAMAN'S CLOAK

Shamanism

All primitive peoples, had certain individuals, called shamans by ethnologists, who had unusual and supernatural powers. Among the tribes of the Northwest Coast there were both men and women shamans. Their extraordinary powers were believed by the Indians to come from supernatural beings who, at particular times, possessed the shaman and spoke through him. Among the Haida and Tlingit a powerful shaman had a considerable number of spirit helpers for each of which there was a special mask. When the influence of a particular being was felt, his mask was worn and the shaman spoke the language of that spirit. Among the northern tribes, the calling of the shaman was usually inherited, his power passing later to his nephew. The dying man informed his heir as to the spirits which would inspire him and gave him the necessary instructions.

In the treatment of the sick, a shaman, performing certain rituals saw the cause of the disorder, usually some natural or supernatural object lodged in the body which became visible to him. It may be that the patient had passed behind a shaman who had swallowed his soul. In that case the curing shaman was able to see the sick man's soul. The soul of the patient may have left his body and gone to the graveyard or into the woods. The actual curing required that the foreign object be removed from the body, or that the soul be restored, if it had wandered away. In the first case, sucking was resorted to and the object was produced from the shaman's mouth. In the second, the shaman went to the place where the strayed soul had been seen by him and caught it between his palms. He displayed it and placed it on the patient's head.

Shamans served the community not only in the curing of the sick but some of them were able to foretell events and to see what was happening in distant parts. Every war party included a shaman who through his supernatural knowledge warned of danger and pointed out favorable times and places for attacks. The shaman, by catching or destroying the souls of the enemy, made the killing of their bodies an easy matter. A powerful shaman would be able to tell where a stranded whale was to be found, or to cause their stranding and was also able to influence the run of fish.

His costume was peculiar; his hair was never cut nor dressed in any way. Suspended from his neck he wore a bone head-scratcher and a tube through which he blew on his patients. He also wore a long bone through the septum of his nose. On various occasions, he displayed his power particularly by walking through fire; often he entered into contests with rival shamans when their respective spirit helpers engaged in combat.

Among the northern tribes, when a shaman died, he was buried, not cremated, and supernatural power remained in the vicinity of his grave house which was at a distance from the village. His soul was said to go to a special abode, usually in the sky. Among the Tlingit, shamans rivaled the chiefs in the power exercised over the people.

MODEL REPRESENTING A SHAMAN

WITH RAVEN SYMBOLS.

MODEL OF SHAMAN'S GRAVE

KWAKIUTL CEREMONIAL MASK

Winter Ceremonies

Throughout the Northwest Coast there were secret societies which gave dramatizations of myths during the winter. To the uninitiated, the actors appeared to be possessed by supernatural beings and to perform miracles. From their viewpoint, at least, these ceremonies were chiefly religious. Those who were engaged in the performances prepared the properties, rehearsed with care, and endeavored to act so realistically as to deceive their audiences. These occasions were dramatic, or theatrical, however, since the presentations were dramatizations of the acts of supernatural mythical beings, or manifestations of present-day supernatural power, the religious element may be considered as predominating.

These winter ceremonies were in their main features common over the entire area. They were begun at a rather definite moment when supernatural beings and powers were thought to arrive and remain in the villages. The moment of their arrival was announced by the sound of whistles which, in theory at least, the uninitiated thought was made by the spirits of the winter ceremony. These whistles were heard during the ceremony whenever those possessed of some supernatural spirit were present or were performing. Since feasting and distribution of property were constantly taking place at this time of the year, the social features were especially pronounced. The events were planned and controlled by the nobility since only this class was able to provide the necessary food and gifts.

Kwakiutl Ceremonies. A description of one of the ceremonies of a Kwakiutl secret society will give some idea of the nature of these rituals. The annual ceremony was initiated by an announcement made by some man that he wished his son to assume membership in the society to which he held a right. This privilege of membership was usually secured through marriage. A man's father-in-law at the time of the marriage promised to give him his place in a secret society. This membership, however, was generally held in trust for the children of the newly married couple. When a son was of proper age to assume his membership his father asked that the promise be fulfilled. At this time also the father-in-law returned to his son-in-law the payment made at the time of the marriage, with additional property, often four or five times the value he received for his daughter. The chiefs consulted to make sure that the man and his relatives had sufficient wealth to carry through the ceremony properly. The whole tribe was convened and notice given of the prospective ceremony. The winter dance pole was brought in and the man and his father-in-law announced the amount of property to be transferred. The people were directed to purify themselves during the succeeding four days by bathing in the sea in the early morning. After the bath, they rubbed themselves with hemlock branches. All relations between the sexes must cease because the spirits of the winter ceremonies were about to come to the village and human odors are offensive to them. As the assembly dispersed, the young man who was about to take his place in the society disappeared with a characteristic cry. The people were reminded that he had been taken by the cannibal spirit to his home in the north where he would be initiated by the supernatural people living there. He was expected back at the end of four days at which time the people were requested to reassemble.

The house of the winter ceremonies was cleared out and prepared for the celebrations. After four days had passed, the people were summoned to this house by special messengers. It will be remembered that when the northwestern people came to a feast or formal assembly they were always seated according to rank by clans, families, septs, tribes, etc. During the winter ceremony, however, they were grouped according to the societies to which they belonged. These societies fell into two main divisions, the more important called the seal society was composed of all the dancing or drama-acting bodies. The various societies forming the seals are graded in importance, at their head being the *hamatsa* or cannibal society. The less important division also consisted of graded societies bearing animal names in which the people were grouped according to sex and age. Between these two groups existed much rivalry and assumed enmity. Not only were the people differently grouped during the winter ceremony, but each individual had a special name by which he had to be called during this period. This was no doubt, a recognition of what was believed to be a changed or different personality. The various societies arrived at the house in groups and were assigned seats together. The seal society came in last and was seated at the rear of the house with the cannibal society in the place of highest honor. The master of ceremonies circled the fire singing and swinging his rattle. The assembled people sang, each individual singing his own secret song.

KWAKIUTL MASKS

KWAKIUTL CEREMONIAL MASKS

HAIDAS IN CEREMONIAL COSTUME

THE BODY OF CHIEF SHAKES LYING IN STATE AND BELOW A SCENE FROM A THEATRICAL ENTERTAINMENT COMMEMORATIVE OF THE LEGEND OF THE ALLIANCE OF CHIEF SHAKES WITH THE BEAR FAMILY.

Other men took this opportunity to have children initiated so that the ceremony was repeated as many times as there were novices.

There were feasts at night and, during the next three days, much singing and dancing. Meantime, the father-in-law turned over the promised property to his son-in-law, the father of the boy who was absent with the supernatural ones being initiated by them. The third evening those who had previously been initiated were called to an assembling place in the woods where they were taught new songs by the singing masters who composed them. The novice and his assistant, a kinswoman, were nearby in the woods, listening, so that they would be able to dance to the songs when the ceremony was held.

The people of the village were formally called to the assembly house soon after dark. The messengers entered each house in the village and called the names of the inmates in the order of their society rank. When they had assembled, individuals came in, one after the other and performed one of the dances which they possessed. At the door were heralds who announced the dancers. There was much fun and good-natured raillery. Occasionally, messengers were sent out to see if the novice were returning. Toward morning the ghost dancer appeared and his song was sung. The older members of the *hamatsa* society suddenly entered the house from both ends and through the roof. They cried "Hap hap" and danced around the fire four times in a squatting position. The novice was supposed to be attracted by their cries. He was heard on the roof, and after running around four times, he pushed a roof plank aside three times, and the fourth time, jumped down. While some tried to catch him he ran around the fire four times and disappeared through a secret door in the rear of the house, leaving behind him the hemlock branches which were his clothing. He entered and disappeared three times and then the assembly was dismissed.

After a short rest the people were assembled on the beach, where joining hands, they formed a square, and tried to surround the novice who appeared, then disappeared, only to appear suddenly again at a distant and unexpected place. The fourth time he was caught through the device of placing a naked man in front of him; the novice rushed up to him and bit his arm. The kinswoman helper who had been in the woods with him during the four days now appeared and danced into the house backward to lure the novice in. After much delay, he entered and rushed about, biting the arms of different people. He repeatedly fled to a room in the rear of the house which had been provided for him. After much singing and dancing he was restored to his senses.

Later, in private, a few of the leaders purified the newly initiated man and his female attendant. The property received from his father-in-law by the man giving the ceremony was publicly distributed. Payment had to be made to all persons bitten by the "cannibal." Incidentally, there were minor initiations and much supplementary feasting.

Ordinarily, there were initiations, similar to the one outlined above, given by other groups resident in the village or temporarily there as guests. Each had its own ceremony, differing from the others

DANCING TO RESTORE AN ECLIPSED MOON

in minor details. When given together there was much rivalry to see which group could give the most spectacular and mystifying performance.

In theory, the cannibal novice, while absent, had become accustomed to eating corpses. It is said that formerly his woman attendant enticed him into the assembly house by holding in front of him a corpse secured from the nearby village burial place. The candidate was said to have eaten the dried skin from the body and to have been joined in his feasting by the older members of the society. Often there would be contests to see which group had a cannibal society member who could outdo the others in corpse-eating. There are also accounts of slaves being killed to supply fresh food for the cannibals. The biting and pretended eating of dogs caught up alive was the more common indication of frenzy shown by the northern tribes.

Magical Performances. During the ceremonies at night in the assembly house there were many exhibitions of sleight-of-hand. A common trick was for a woman who had great supernatural power to invite someone to run her through with a spear or to cut off her head. A shaman restored her and took her underground in spite of all attempts to hold her. During one such exhibition a woman was struck by a paddle which seemed to cleave her shoulder well down to her breast. Blood was seen to flow in abundance. These performances were, of course, arranged in advance and executed with the aid of confederates. The head displayed as severed was realistically

TSIMSHIAN DANCERS

71

carved of wood. The blood which flowed was enclosed in a bladder and was released by the blow. The spear supposed to be thrust through the body telescoped; and, by means of a string attached to the skin, it could be made to appear that the point of the spear raised the skin on the opposite side of the body. The corpse eating described above, no doubt, belonged also with these sleight-of-hand performances. Under the circumstances it is difficult to know how much of religious attitude and belief there was on the part of the initiated who planned and carried out the winter ceremonies. It is probable that they did believe that the candidate was in some degree possessed by the cannibal spirit and that those who appeared in masks were temporarily acting as substitutes for the supernatural beings themselves. The deliberate deceptions were to impress the uninitiated by greatly exaggerating the display of supernatural power which was sincerely believed to exist in less evident forms.

Potlatch

The word "potlatch" comes from the Chinook jargon and originally meant "to give." In its common use among the white people and the natives on the Northwest Coast it has taken on a very general meaning and applied to any Indian festival at which there is feasting, or, in connection with which property is given away. Because of this loose and general meaning there necessarily exists a good deal of confusion as to what is meant by the term. From the Indian's viewpoint many different things are meant when he uses

KWAKIUTL MASKED DANCERS

the Chinook word in speaking to white people, for it is the only word intelligible to them by means of which he can refer to a considerable number of ceremonies or festivals each having its own Indian name.

In the potlatch there are perhaps two main principles involved: first that all events of social or political interest must be publicly witnessed; and second that those who perform personal or social service must be publicly recompensed. A third more general social law is that all guests on all occasions must be fed. If we may judge from the more widely distributed aspects of the ceremonies of the various tribes along the coast, potlatches were primarily the accompaniment of certain crises in the life of an individual.

A child under a year old was not called by name but was referred to by the place of its birth. When it was a year old a name was given it and presents of a mat or paddle were made to its relatives. At ten or twelve a boy received another name and there was a greater distribution of property. The girls reached maturity at a somewhat more advanced age, at which time among the Nootka a very important feast with a lavish distribution of property took place. At a less definite age the boy was initiated into the secret society to which he had an inherited or an acquired claim. This was also an event of great importance among the southern tribes. As has been described above, betrothal and marriage were also potlatch occasions. Of still greater importance was the ceremony at which the father-in-law made return gifts, which usually took place some years after the marriage.

Among the northern tribes, Haida, Tlingit, and Tsimshian, the main potlatch occasion occurred after the death of an important person when the final burial rites were held, the remains entombed, and a memorial to the dead erected. The burial duties devolved upon the family of the father of the deceased, connected of course with the opposite, or at least a different clan. At the time of the ceremony those who attended to the burial were recompensed. At this time, moreover, there were exhibitions of dancing by the other members of the clan of the deceased and a distribution of property to them also.

The building of a house required the hiring of various individuals who secured the timbers and assisted in putting them in place and in the ornamentation of the house with carvings and paintings. The potlatch has often been confused with the winter ceremonies which were the occasions for initiations into the secret societies.

One prominent feature of all the events just enumerated was the assumption of a new name by the giver of the feast. This always meant an advance in standing and rank and was perhaps the strongest motive behind the whole potlatch system.

Since all these occasions required the dispensing of hospitality, considerable supplies of food were necessary and were accumulated by unusual activities in fishing and food gathering on the part of the man and his family, or, in recent years, by the purchase of provisions from traders with money received as wages. The second requisite was a supply of presents for distribution. These formerly consisted of slaves, canoes, and clothing, especially skins. More recently, the gray Hudson Bay blankets superseded nearly all other forms of prop-

NOOTKA DANCING MASK

GREASE DISH. TLINGIT

73

erty. These blankets could, of course, also be accumulated through purchase from the traders as a result of thrift. Such blankets when given away were not ordinarily used as apparel, but were hoarded as a sort of currency. Although an individual was the principal figure in a potlatch, it was not entirely a personal matter. His family and relatives were also interested and bound by tradition to assist in making it a success. They were drawn upon for blankets which might be returned to them later.

When property was publicly distributed it fell into two categories, as payment for services rendered, or as compensation for injuries. This was a limited transaction and the obligation was cancelled. The greater amount of property was given to invited guests, to each according to his rank. Such gifts could be declined and became binding obligations upon the recipient and his heirs, so that when he in turn gave a potlatch, he had to re-pay more than an equivalent to this man, or his heirs. In this second case, giving was really profitable lending. Among the Kwakiutl such forced lending was not confined to public occasions. If a man were planning to give a potlatch, he lent his stock of blankets some months before the event and collected them again with considerable interest.

The main purpose of the potlatch may be assumed to have been the impression made on the public mind. It was this which elevated the man and his family in the public estimation. The more widely the invitations were sent out, the more spectacular the display of property, and the more lavish the feasting, the greater and deeper was the emotional result and the longer did it endure. To increase this effect the property was publicly displayed on the beach. As a permanent record, posts were erected at either end of the long piles of blankets. Often too, in more recent years, inscriptions were placed over the man's door and added to his grave monument so that the event would not be forgotten.

The After Life

The most characteristic belief among the tribes of the Northwest Coast in regard to the fate of souls after death was that it depended upon the kind of death by which they were freed. The larger number, those who died of old age or disease, went toward the west and had to cross water barriers, usually rivers. There was some disagreement whether the world of dead was on the same level as this or below it. Life in that world was similar to this, but much less agreeable. To some extent the souls depended on their surviving relatives for food and clothing. The latter was chiefly supplied at the time of the funeral, but food was sent frequently by placing it in the fire.

Shaman's souls also went to a special place — according to the Haida, an island. Certain of the shaman's powers continued an association with the body which, it will be remembered, was given a different sort of burial from that accorded an ordinary person.

A second death was believed to be possible so that the soul passed from the first place of the dead to another, either below the first or farther to the west. Some of the souls, perhaps the majority, were reborn, usually in the same family to which they belonged in the first instance.

WAR CLUB AND LADLE. KWAKIUTL

The Bella Coola believed that at death three separate entities survived. One of these went above to the House of Myths, a second to the world of the dead, below this world, and a third part manifested itself here in the hooting of the owl.

Mythology and Folklore

The myths of a people are generally assumed to be a formulation of their beliefs in the supernatural origins of the world and of mankind and his social institutions, that is, they are a system of belief which explains the world as it is. In so far as they treat of the supernatural they may be viewed as religious in character. But in addition to accounts of the creation of the world, of a flood, and other momentous events, there are usually found many trivial and ludicrous narratives and incidents. It is evident that the creative imagination of mankind has been at work and the gods and heroes are made to furnish amusement by their adventures and pranks. We are dealing then, to a certain extent, with unwritten literature rather than with religion. In North American mythology there are a number of characters who are at the same time gods and tricksters.

Raven Myths. The chief mythological character on the North Pacific Coast was Raven. The people lived close to the shore and ravens were always about, the most intimate and sociable of man's animal neighbors. It is noticeable that there was an attempt to sublimate the raven's personal characteristics by representing the mythical hero as simply wearing a raven's robe at times and assuming his form as a disguise. The Tlingit distinguished the hero as the Raven of the head of Nass River, a being distinct from the common bird. There can be no doubt, however, that the real bird has contributed much to the conception of the hero's personality and has suggested many of the grotesque incidents. This is particularly apparent in many episodes in which his voracious appetite is the main motive.

In the beginning, according to the Haida, the sea covered all the world, except a flat rock on which the supernatural ones lay crisscross. Raven alighted among these beings and then flew to the top of the sky through which he was able to pass. Arriving in the upper world, he displaced the chief's infant grandson. Soon after, he was dropped from his cradle and fell into the sea. A messenger invited him to a house under the water where he was given two cylindrical objects and directions for using them to make land. He bungled the matter somewhat, but the objects given him first expanded to form the Queen Charlotte Islands and then the mainland.

Among other adventures, Raven was befriended by Beavers who had a lake filled with fish and a salmon trap for catching them. Raven, taking advantage of the absence of his hosts, rolled up the lake, fish, and fishtrap and carried them away in his armpit. By this means people secured the use of fish as food. After this, Raven fell in with Eagle and, by trickery, took from him a basket of fresh water. As Eagle chased him, Raven spilled the water here and there, making the fresh water lakes and streams, also necessary that there might be fish for food. Later he got eulachon from their supernatural owner and keeper by pretending that his canoe was already smeared with eulachon grease and spawn, and distributed them at the various

KWAKIUTL DANCER

KWAKIUTL DANCER

places where the fish are now plentiful. By changing himself into a conifer needle and floating on the drinking water he procured his birth as a child of the chief's daughter. He cried perpetually for daylight which was kept in a box by the chief until his grandfather ordered that it be given him to quiet him. Resuming his bird shape, he flew through the smoke-hole with the box and later placed the stars, moon, and sun in the sky. He secured fire by appearing among the animals at the house of the guardian of fire in the form of a deer. He tied faggots to his tail and, when the opportunity offered, set these on fire and ran out. By switching his tail against the trees he made them capable of supporting fire.

He tried to make an old woman who held the tide-line believe he had already gathered sea urchins. He blinded her and made her promise to let the tides run out twice a day instead of at much longer intervals. This made the clam digging and gathering of low-tide food possible.

At one time also he caused the waters to rise, making a flood, escaping himself by means of an arrow chain. He shot the first arrow into the sky and each succeeding one into the nock of the preceding one until he was able to climb up to the sky.

He gave the birds their various colors by painting them. His own blackness was due to his being caught in the smoke-hole of a house and being subjected to prolonged smoking.

Besides the beneficent deeds mentioned above, there were a great number of other exploits, some of which seem intended to show what might be done with unlimited magical power. There were also many in which Raven satisfied his appetite for food or sexual gratification, making use of all sorts of tricks in order to accomplish his ends.

Family Traditions. Besides those commonly known to the entire community, there were many myths and traditions connected with particular families and considered to be their private property. They were intended to account for the high standing of the family and its right to the use of houses, house furniture, certain personal names, and various ceremonial possessions. The narrative might be the bare outline of the migrations of the early ancestors. In a Kwakiutl tale, the First One, a whale, traveled in his whale canoe until he came to a desirable place, where he disembarked and built a house with certain peculiarities and having a certain name. The ancestor continued his journey, marrying the daughters of many chiefs and constantly obtaining new names and rights which became hereditary. The fortunes of the family were traced down to the present and justified its claim to recognition. Another type of Kwakiutl story usually concerns a young man of early times, who, after many purifications arrived at a house into which he is invited. The door was alive and opened and shut; the house posts were also alive and talked; or a woman was grown to the floor in the house. Sometimes, as a result of marriage, but at times without, the young man was given the house with its contents, the personal names of the owner, and his ceremonial masks, songs, and dances.

As an example of one of these myths which explains the history and possessions of a group, the following abstract may be of interest. It concerns the Kwakiutl sept, Wiwomasgem.

A Thunderbird named, Too-large, suggested to his wife that they go down to the world beneath them. They did so and came to the mouth of a river where a man named Only-one-on-the-beach was building a house, unassisted. Thunderbird and his wife removed their masks, appeared in human form, and took the names, Head-winter-dancer and Head-winter-dance-woman. When Only-one-on-the-Beach's house was finished, he assisted the visitors in the building of their house on a hill near a river. Here, in a short time, four sons were born to the couple. These boys grew up with magical rapidity and were established in houses of their own at some distance from each other. For the fourth son, Head-winter-dancer, called down his own house from the upper world and presented it to him with a number of masks and the names and dances belonging with them.

TSIMSHIAN DANCERS

Head-winter-dancer had made himself a salmon weir with a trap to hold the salmon. One morning he found in the trap a mysterious salmon which, after some treatment, took its proper form, that of the two-headed serpent. Just at this time a fifth son was born. When the baby was washed, blood from the serpent was put on it and the parts so treated turned to stone, until the boy, now twice the size of an ordinary man, was all stone except for his neck at least, on the surface. His mother then recognized him as the offspring of Dzonoqwa, a supernatural being who had visited her during a fainting fit. The boy destined to be a warrior was named Stone-body.

This man, of double stature and largely composed of stone, could not travel in an ordinary canoe. His father then remembered that a self-propelling canoe named Paddleside-serpent-canoe had been promised him by Only-one-on-the-beach in payment for curing his sons of frogs which had infested their stomachs. This canoe proved to be the proper means of transportation for Stone-body. First he was taken to the houses of his four brothers and introduced to them by his father. After that he set out to make war on the whole world, to secure slaves, wealth, names, and dances for his brothers. The canoe transported him and his slaves at a word of command.

When he appeared near a village his shout killed or rendered insensible all the men, except the chief of the village, who immediately bought off Stone-body with slaves, skins of animals, and names with their prerogatives. These, Stone-body transferred to his brothers. Finally, Stone-body went south to Comox, a Salish settlement near Cape Mudge. Here he secured the ceremony of the earthquake (Xwexwe). After his return, he went up a certain river, very dangerous because of its water monsters, to secure eagle down. At a certain place, he was attacked by two brothers of his elder brother's wife, sons of one of Stone-body's victims. They succeeded in destroying the Paddleside-serpent-canoe and in killing the crew and Stone-body himself. They had been told he was vulnerable in his neck, the only part of his body not turned to stone. The heads taken as trophies were carried to the village of the two brothers where they were discovered by their sister on one of her visits to her former home. When Stone-body's relatives came for revenge, they were all killed by the two brothers who had great supernatural power.

This story, many of the details having been omitted here, explains various names of the important people in this Kwakiutl sept, why they have houses with certain carved posts and the ownership of the salmon rivers, and how they came to have the right to certain masks and dances.

FEAST DISH (DOUBLE-HEADED SERPENT) AND CEREMONIAL CURTAIN

TLINGIT CHILKAT BLANKETS

SAMPLES OF SPRUCE
ROOT WEAVING

ARGILLITE CARVING

NOOTKA BASKETS

Textile Decoration. The development of the embellishment of objects of utility, in any one region is largely dependent upon the general industries practised there. On the Northwest Coast pottery was entirely lacking, and clay, the material most readily modeled, was not employed as an artistic medium. The household vessels were mostly made of wood; carving of wood therefore, was the most prominent art manifestation. In the south, among the Salish and in the north, among the Tlingit, basketry was well developed, but in the main central portion of the area, except for the hats, the baskets were crude and used for gathering and carrying clams and similar work for which decorated basketry was unsuitable. Mats, however, were common to the entire area. On them we find the simple, geometric, decorative designs inherent in textile technique where the elements employed cross at right angles to each other. There were brown or black stripes; solid, or with alternating stitches of background and color. Squares and rectangles were also employed as design units. The Salish blankets and some very old examples from the northern tribes have similar decorations. Also formerly among the northern tribes porcupine quill embroidery quite naturally lent itself to the same sort of geometrical ornamentation.

We find, then, on the Pacific Coast, one type of art, which is common to the rest of North America. Nearly everywhere textiles were made by women; consequently, their decoration was entirely the artistic expression of women. On the Northwest Coast, where there was no pottery and where clothing was scanty, women's contribution to decorative art was rather limited.

Carving. The men on the other hand, built the canoes, erected the houses, manufactured the implements employed in fishing and hunting, and provided the wooden dishes for household use. Unconstrained as it was by the limitations of the textile technique, the decorative art of the men inclined more toward realistic and grotesque representations than did that of the women. On the Northwest Coast the chief artistic expressions were through carving in the round and in relief, or through painting. The materials used for carving were wood, bone, horn, and, more recently, slate. As has been mentioned above, the Indians of this area were fortunate in the character of the available wood. The cedars are soft, straight, and fine grained and the large alders supply wood very suitable for carving with primitive implements.

The products of the women were, on the other hand, severely hampered by reason of the limitations imposed by the media. In the representative carvings and paintings of the men there was

KNIVES AND CARVING TOOLS

ARGILLITE CHEST

NOOTKA POLE

considerable opportunity for variation in form and composition, though they were naturally guided to some extent by traditional concepts of the forms portrayed. The emotions aroused in the beholders may be stirred by suggestion, through memory associations. Ordinarily, the emotional result of an artistic work is in large measure dependent upon the responses it elicits in the mind of the beholder. The better carvers of the Northwest Coast were skilful enough to portray accurately features of religious and symbolic significance. Some of the grave monuments were executed in that spirit. On the other hand, some carvings were definitely intended as realistic representations of animals and portraits of humans, rather than as representations of mythical monsters and personages.

Realistic art was not common on the Pacific Coast for two reasons. In a great many cases where the object carved was for a ceremonial use the animals were not realistic representations of the familiar ones of everyday life. They were either mythical beings belonging to the supernatural past or present, or were the actual animals represented in the more nearly human form, which they were all believed to possess. In the second place, the totem poles in particular were intended to suggest a narrative, or a combination of ideas. To do this the artist took liberties with the anatomy of the animals in order to bring about the combination he desired.

Art. It is the first motive mentioned before that was responsible for much of the grotesque nature of the art of the Northwest Coast. The Kwakiutl, for example, represented a mysterious "woman" of the woods and tried to produce in her likeness the mystery and fear which the belief in her inspired. The many masks used in the ceremonies were intended to and did produce feelings of horror and dread especially in the children. The object of the ceremonies was to magnify the power of the initiated who were believed either to be aided by the monsters represented, or to be actually these beings themselves. The double-headed snake was one of the most powerful of the supernatural helpers. Such an unnatural creature would arouse more awe than elicited by the representation of a snake. In general, the Northwest Coast concept of supernatural power combined a considerable degree of horror and fear. A good example is the cannibal spirit represented as feeding on human corpses. The concept was no less repellent to Indians than to us, and accounts for the feeling of the supernatural at the time of the ceremony.

Totem Poles. Examples of connected narratives in Northwest Coast carvings were not very numerous, but they did occur on totem poles where some carving on the pole served as a memory device to recall some mythological incident. More generally it was desired to

NOOTKA POLE

GRAVEYARD BAY POLE —

SKIDEGATE VILLAGE

represent the main crests belonging to the family. These may have been two, three, or four, belonging to the man and his wife, and occupied prominent positions at the top, bottom, and middle of the pole. They were joined and the remaining space occupied by the representation of conventionalized animal forms, etc. It was often desired to represent animals as the ancestors of the family upon these poles and they were, therefore, shown with human faces and were distinguished from each other with difficulty.

Certain features of animals were selected as symbols and with these in mind, as keys, the figures may usually be identified. Animals were distinguished from humans by placing their ears at the top of their heads. Birds were recognized by their beaks, imposed often on an otherwise human face. Fish were indicated either by gills or fins. The three most common birds, raven, eagle, and hawk, may be distinguished by the shape of the beak: straight for the raven, curved for the eagle, and curved until the tip rests on the mouth or chin for the hawk. Of land mammals, the beaver was represented in full by large incisor teeth, a scaly flat tail, and a stick held to his mouth with his forepaws. The grizzly bear was indicated by a large mouth full of teeth, a protruding tongue, and large paws. The killer-whale, found many times and under a great variety of conditions, was symbolized by the dorsal fin and generally also by a blow hole. Of the fishes the shark was recognized by a vaulted forehead on which are three crescents. The sculpin, in addition to gills, had two spines over its mouth.

Besides these natural animals, often shown in a human or super-natural phase, there were supernatural beings, or personified natural objects. The moon, for instance, was often shown with a circular face which resembled a hawk. The mythical thunderbird did not differ much from an eagle. If the bird were shown as bearing off a whale, the first was certainly intended. A water monster might appear in a variety of forms sometimes resembling a bear or a beaver.

It appears that heraldic and mythological art can have its full effect only when those who view it are entirely familiar with the stories and concepts which lie behind it. Since, in many cases, these myths of family origin were not fully known except to the members of the family, they alone were capable of receiving the full emotional value. To some extent then the art was esoteric.

Carved Ornamentation. We may consider that the primary object of house posts, totem poles, and memorial columns was to present graphic representations of varying and related concepts. If we consider other objects, such as dishes, spoons, clubs, etc., the carving becomes secondary and must supplement its use. Feast dishes

KAISUN VILLAGE 1901   KWAKIUTL INSIDE HOUSE POST

BELLA COOLA HOUSE

PAINT BRUSHES

DOUBLE MASK: CLOSED, RAVEN AS A BIRD; OPEN, RAVEN AS A MAN

MOON AND MOUNTAIN GOAT STORAGE BOXES

DECORATING HAT

INSIDE HOUSE POST — TANOO, Q.C.IS.

DOGFISH FRONTAL BOARD OFF   MORTUARY POLE   SKEDANS, Q.C.IS.

HAIDA ARGILLITE PIPE

HAWK DESIGN RATTLE

HAWK DESIGN DISH FROM GOAT HORN

FISH FLOAT

TSIMSHIAN FROG LADLE

possessed names and were conceived as animate. They were carved in human or animal form with a bowl in the back or belly according to the posture chosen. Smaller oil dishes were often made to represent a seal, in which case a fairly realistic head or face was carved at one end and a tail at the other. The flippers were also sometimes represented on the two sides. The natural proportions of the animal, however, were subsidiary to the form imposed by the requirements of its use as a vessel. Bowls of mountain goat horn were given very effective representative appearances by means of low relief carving. Spoon handles were somewhat more difficult because of their tapering shape; but when once the habit of decorating has been established, and the principle of representation by parts has been adopted, many obstacles can be successfully overcome.

It is generally conceded that the Northwest Coast peoples did not smoke tobacco until Europeans introduced the habit about 125 years ago. Within that time the Tlingit and Haida have carried over the carving habit from the making of spoons and rattles to pipe-making, and have produced a variety of forms.

Rearrangements and Dissections. So far, we have illustrated and discussed carving by men in the round or in high relief. The square

HAIDA MASKS AND RATTLES

BELLA COOLA GRAVE

SCULPIN CARVING   KWAKIUTL

TATTOO DESIGN OF WATER MONSTER   HAIDA

boxes made by folding a single straight board, as described above, also offered opportunities for decoration. These were usually carved in low relief and further embellished with color. As in the case of the dishes dug out of a single piece, it was feasible to carve the front aspect of the animal on one end, and on its rear parts the opposite end, and on the sides, the sides of the animal's body. Still greater freedom was taken in this case with the relative sizes and relations of the body parts. The liberties taken in these respects seem to have moved along these lines of altered proportions and of an analysis of anatomical parts amounting to actual dissection. Frequently an animal was shown as if it were split from the rear to the nose and spread out into two profiles joined in front only. Examples may be seen in bracelets where the two parts of the longitudinally bisected animal encircled the wrist. Paintings on a plane surface were also treated in this manner, where no evident obstacle had been the compelling cause. In the bear split down the back and spread open as a painted decoration on a Tsimshian house front, it seems probable that the bilateral natural symmetry of the animal has been utilized by the artist to give a symmetrical treatment around the house entrance through the bear's navel.

Symmetry. We have been dealing with neither realistic, nor plain symbolic art, but with a representative art which relies for its effectiveness chiefly upon associative memory. We discussed above the end result of a problem of composition and symmetry. Here the artist employs painting and low relief carving in which the elements of design are body parts treated with great freedom as to their arrangement. The composition was adapted to the shape of the sur-

KILLER-WHALE DESIGN CLUB   TLINGIT

CARVED WOLF AND PAINTED KILLER WHALE BOW DESIGN

90

MASKS OF SUPERNATURAL BEINGS   BELLA COOLA

MISC. DESIGNS

BEAVER

DOGFISH

BEAVER

SCULPIN

CHILKAT BLANKET

face available for decoration; the shape and relative size of body parts were adjusted to give pleasing lines. Angles gave way to curves, natural disproportions were equalized, and by the use of wider and narrower lines, or varying color, the desired results were obtained. So conventionalized had this art of dissected and freely arranged animal parts become, that the artist cut out patterns of eyes or fins and used them in drawing the outlines of his designs. Art of this sort was found on house fronts, settee backs, canoes, paddles, ends and side of boxes, skin robes, and the woven blankets of the Chilkat.

We have then on the Northwest Coast, a woman's geometric decorative art of a textile origin, similar to that found generally in North America; a man's realistic and representative art, in which the weird and mysterious are often represented; and finally, as an outgrowth of this, an elaborate conventionalized art in which body parts have been distorted from their natural anatomical form and have been given other fixed proportions according to the esthetic requirements imposed by the form of the object to be decorated.

SHIRT DESIGN   TLINGIT

TATTOO DESIGN: WHALE MONSTER WITH WOLF'S HEAD   HAIDA

DANCING APRON   TLINGIT

SPLIT-APART SHARK DESIGN   HAIDA

HOUSE FRONT DESIGN

KWAKIUTL VILLAGE

SOME FURTHER REFERENCES

ABUNDANT RIVERS, by Anthony Carter, Hancock House Publishers, Saanichton, B.C. 1972

ARCHAEOLOGY OF THE GULF OF GEORGIA AND PUGET SOUND, by Harlan I. Smith, American Museum of Natural History, Vol. 4, Part 6, 1907

ART OF THE KWAKIUTL INDIANS AND OTHER NORTHWEST COAST TRIBES, by Audrey Hawthorne, University of British Columbia, Vancouver, B.C.

ART OF THE NORTHWEST COAST INDIANS, by R.B. Inverarity, University of California Press, Berkeley, 1950.

ARTIFACTS OF THE NORTHWEST COAST INDIANS, by Hilary Stewart, Hancock House Publishers, Saanichton, B.C., 1973.

ARTS OF THE RAVEN, by Wilson Duff, Bill Holm, and Bill Reid, Catalogue Vancouver Art Gallery, 1967.

BRITISH COLUMBIA HERITAGE SERIES: OUR NATIVE PEOPLES, British Columbia Department of Education, Victoria, B.C., Vol. 1, Introduction to Our Native Peoples, Vol. 4, Haida.

CONTRIBUTIONS TO THE ETHNOLOGY OF THE HAIDA, by J.R. Swanton, Jesup North Pacific Expedition, American Museum of Natural History, Vol. 5, 1905.

HAIDA MYTHS ILLUSTRATED IN ARGILLITE CARVINGS, by Marius Barbeau, National Museum of Canada, Ottawa, 1953.

INDIAN CANOES OF THE NORTHWEST COAST, by Bill Durham, Copper Canoe Press, Seattle, 1960.

INDIAN PRIMITIVE, by Ralph W. Andrews, Crown Publishers, New York.

INDIANS OF THE NORTHWEST COAST, by Phillip Drucker, Anthropological Handbook #10, American Museum of Natural History, Mcgraw-Hill 1955.

INDIANS OF THE PACIFIC NORTHWEST, by Ruth Underhill, U.S. Department of the Interior, Bureau of Indian Affairs, Washington, D.C. 1945.

MONUMENTS IN CEDAR, by Edward L. Keithahn, Superior Publishing Co., Seattle, Washington, 1963.

MY HEART SOARS, by Chief Dan George and Helmut Hirnschall, Hancock House Publishers, Saanichton, B.C. 1974.

THE NORTH AMERICAN INDIAN, Edward S. Curtis, several volumes and Folio. Norwood 1915.

NORTHWEST COAST INDIAN ART, by Bill Holm, University of Washington Press, Seattle, 1965.

PRIMITIVE ART, by Franz Boas, Dover Publications, New York, 1955.

SOMEWHERE BETWEEN, by Anthony Carter, Hancock House Publishers, Saanichton, B.C. 1966.

SPIRIT IN STONE: Petroglyphs of the Northwest Coast Indians, by Beth and Ray Hill, Hancock House Publishers, Saanichton, B.C. 1974.

THIS IS HAIDA, by Anthony Carter, Hancock House Publishers, Saanichton, B.C. 1966.

THOSE BORN AT KOONA, by John and Carolyn Smyly, Hancock House Publishers Saanichton, B.C. 1973.

TOTEM POLES, by Marius Barbeau, Vols. I & 11, National Museum of Canada Bulletin 119, Ottawa 1950.

TOTEM POLES OF THE GITKSAN, UPPER SKEENA RIVER, by Marius Barbeau, National Museum of Canada, Ottawa, 1961.

TSIMSHIAN MYTHS, by Marius Barbeau, National Museum of Canada, Ottawa, 1961.

THE WOLF AND THE RAVEN, by Viola E. Garfield, and Linn A. Forrest, University of Washington Press, Seattle, 1948.

images stone b.c.

THIRTY CENTURIES OF NORTHWEST COAST INDIAN SCULPTURE

WILSON DUFF

IMAGES: STONE: B.C.

By Wilson Duff and Hilary Stewart

192 pp., 9 x 8 ins.,
200 photographs and sketches.
Hardcover $14.95   *ISBN 0-919654-27-4*
Softcover $7.95   *ISBN 0-919654-29-0*

my heart soars

by Chief Dan George
with Illustrations by Helmut Hirnschall

Chief Dan George has been described as a logger, musician, film and television star, philosopher and a man who speaks for all Indians.

His concern for the young people in modern society finds as much expression as his love for children. He advises them how to adjust to the white man's world and how to maintain their heritage. He pleads with the old . . . "remember, so that the young will listen."

Drawings and sketches supply the visual art, depicting native people, animals and scenes of the magnificent wilderness.

96 pages, 8 x 9 in.
ISBN 0-919654-15-0
Library of Congress
Catalog Card 74-78350
To be published September
hard cover $9.95

The Story of Haida Totems
Those Born At Koona

by John and Carolyn Smyly

A much awaited for contribution to a neglected subject: the meaning of the totem poles of the Queen Charlotte Islands. The reader will be inspired to a deeper understanding of the story tellers, legend bearers and master artists and carvers who created the great totem — the Sea Grizzly, Eagles, Raven and more — many of which are now but decaying, moss covered totems or museum specimens.

Have you ever gazed quickly at a totem pole? Wondered what it was saying? Contemplated what its crests meant? Or wondered how it fitted into the structure of a village? THOSE BORN AT KOONA draws together as complete a story as will ever be told about these monuments of cedar.

Twenty years of research, first commissioned by the British Columbian Provincial Museum, into historical documents, old museum collections, early explorers' journals and many trips to the now abandoned village site, have resulted in the unique portrayal and description of every known totem of Skedans. The book contains more than 50 historical photographs and 70 illustrations of Skedans village, once called Koona.

120 pages, 8 x 11 in.
ISBN 0-919654-03-7
Library of Congress Catalog Card Number 73-84988
Hard Bound